"Ed's book is, indeed, a treasure! You will feel instantly that he is your friend and fellow traveler on this magical journey to your own magical self! Ed writes from his heart with words that stream from the vast capacity of his ever-searching mind. If your life, like mine, is far too busy, this is the book for you. It comes in small 'bites' that can be read and savored in those spare minutes when you want to be entertained, encouraged, energized, and excited. Take it with you and you will find a new friend, counselor, and companion at your side."

—Jane Macgruder Watkins, coauthor with Bernard Mohr of *Appreciative Inquiry: Change at the Speed of Imagination*

"Warm, wise and witty! Reading Ed Jacobson's *Appreciative Moments* is like sitting at the table with your favorite uncle. It rubs off on you, the way wisdom or maturity or the company of a kind mentor does. Each day that you read, you feel yourself a bit wiser, a bit warmer, more full of good humor. This is truly a generous book, one that feels like a gift in each moment you read it. I love this book for the richness of its meaning, for its connections to the culture we have lived in, but most of all for how it connects you to this wonderful man who has written it."

—George Kinder, CFP®, author of *The Seven Stages of Money Maturity* and *A Song for Hana*

"Ed Jacobson is a wise man who has given *Appreciative Moments* as a gift to the world. He is a master storyteller whose wisdom and humor flow together into a stream that effortlessly finds its way into our lives, refreshing our sense of humanity and possibility. The appreciative approach I am *learning from this book elevates the quality of my experience and connection to those I coach and love.* "

—Susan Bradley, CFP®, founder and president,
Sudden Money Institute®, and author of *Sudden Money*

"I love Ed Jacobson's Appreciative Moments! He offers many gifts and blessings in this special publication, with an eye to focusing on what is precious in our work, our friendships, our families, and our hopes for meaningful lives. Ed's unique ability to weave stories through personal experience and anecdotes is uplifting and inspiring and leaves you wanting more. I encourage all who are looking for more positive connections and messages to read Appreciative Moments. It will touch your heart and feed your soul. "

—Marv Tuttle, CAE, executive director/chief executive
officer, Financial Planning Association (FPA)

"Ed's stories read so comfortably, you'll feel like you're having a series of conversations with a wise and optimistic uncle. In his very down-to-earth manner, he helps us see how everyday situations and challenges hold the seeds of great possibility, if we simply adjust the lens slightly and consider the ways we treat and communicate with one another. At once inspirational and practical, each short chapter gives the reader something to put into use immediately, in no time bringing us to a refreshingly effective new way of seeing and doing things. "

—Susan Turnbull, author of *The Wealth of Your Life*

"Ed Jacobson is 'the real deal.' He is an amazing man ... a complete package of wisdom, wit, and warmth. When it comes to the practices and exercises so clearly described in Appreciative Moments, know that Ed not only 'talks the

talk' but he 'walks the walk.' *Appreciative Moments is a heartfelt collection of humor and insight. It's a must-read for anyone really desiring to live life fully and help others do the same.*"

—Richard Kahler, CFP®, coauthor of *Conscious Finance* and *The Financial Wisdom of Ebenezer Scrooge*

"*In Appreciative Moments, Ed Jacobson packages nuggets of life-changing wisdom in a series of engaging vignettes. Be prepared to be entertained, captivated, and inspired by Ed's creative use of words, skillful storytelling, and practical advice for crafting a life well lived.*"

—Carol Anderson, founder and president of Money Quotient® and coauthor of *Your Clients for Life*

"*Along with your BlackBerry and cell phone, this is the book that people in business should take with them everywhere they go! It's a ready reference for finding out how to embrace every moment at work with authentic optimism—you know, the kind of genuinely upbeat thinking and feeling that seems to move mountains. An antidote for fear and negativity, Ed Jacobson's book will put you in a place of real empowerment. The world of work and business is riddled with a deep sense of inadequacy and weakness. This book turns this world on its end and begins to take us to a place where the positive rules. It's a place where enlightened businesses leaders know they should be. Extremely accessible and always believable, I found Appreciate Moments to be a joyously seductive read—how many books on your business shelf can claim that?*"

—Jim Armstrong, founder and creative director of Good for Business and author of *Beyond the Mission Statement*

"*Ed's book is both a thorough delight and a thoroughly practical guide on the journey of living and working in an appreciative way. He radiates the simple wisdom and joy of connecting with others and appreciating our own experiences, through the art of inquiry about what is good, what is working, and what is possible. Reading his stories is like taking a very scenic, relaxing, and pleasurable river trip in which you find yourself suddenly arriving at an equally grand and beautiful destination. By integrating his practices, I find that I am a better coach, leader, spouse, and friend!*"

—Elizabeth Jetton, CFP®, former board chair, Financial Planning Association (FPA)

"*This book is such a gem! Ed Jacobson depicts the full scope of life's simple beauties, and helps us to stop and smell the roses—for real. He generates both laughter and tears while helping us to be thankful for life's uncomplicated but easily missed profundities. The thing is, though, you will do all of these while both appreciating and inquiring. Perhaps most importantly, you will learn something ... and likely become a better person in the bargain.*"

—Dick Wagner, CFP®, founder of InsideMoney.com and cofounder of the Nazrudin Project

"*This book is a treasure! Take it with you and be entertained, encouraged, energized, and excited.*"

—Jane Macgruder Watkins, coauthor of *Appreciative Inquiry: Change at the Speed of Imagination*

"*Ed Jacobson is an amazing man, and Appreciative Moments is a must-read for anyone desiring to live life fully and help others do the same.*"

—Richard Kahler, CFP®,
coauthor of *The Financial Wisdom of Ebenezer Scrooge*

Appreciative Moments

Appreciative Moments

Stories and Practices for Living and Working Appreciatively

Edward A. Jacobson, Ph.D., M.B.A.

TENACITY PRESS

iUniverse, Inc.
New York Bloomington Shanghai

Appreciative Moments
Stories and Practices for Living and Working Appreciatively

iUniverse books may be ordered through booksellers or by contacting:

iUniverse
1663 Liberty Drive
Bloomington, IN 47403
www.iuniverse.com
1-800-Authors (1-800-288-4677)

Because of the dynamic nature of the Internet, any Web addresses or links contained in this book may have changed since publication and may no longer be valid.

The views expressed in this work are solely those of the author and do not necessarily reflect the views of the publisher, and the publisher hereby disclaims any responsibility for them.

ISBN: 978-0-595-42911-0 (pbk)
ISBN: 978-0-595-71746-0 (cloth)
ISBN: 978-0-595-87248-0 (ebk)

Printed in the United States of America

A Tenacity Press Book

Tenacity Press, founded by Hal Zina Bennett and Susan J. Sparrow in 1992, follows the tenets of a literary cooperative. We join an honored tradition of small publishers who through the centuries have championed the works of fine authors. For more information: www.TenacityPress.org

To Jody,
of course

Contents

Acknowledgments

The acknowledgments section is a wonderful convention, giving an author the opportunity to recognize and thank those who have supported the efforts that went into birthing the book. I love giving thanks and recognition, so much so, you could say that is what *Appreciative Moments* is all about: the power of appreciation and gratitude in our personal and work lives. However, writing this section proved unexpectedly difficult for me. Not because I didn't have enough people to thank, but because once I started, I wasn't sure where to stop. That, too, is the subject of the book: how appreciation begets more appreciation.

Appreciative Moments is my first book. At its core, it's a progress report on the lessons I have learned that I can pass along, and how I am attempting to live my life at age sixty-four. So, it's no exaggeration for me to want to acknowledge everyone who has ever taught me—by word, deed, or counterexample—how to live with kindness, caring, joy, and effectiveness. To do it right, I would have to create an acknowledgments section which would be longer than the text itself.

One must start somewhere, however. And so I will begin with thanking my wonderful wife, Jody, with whom each moment is a teaching moment (by word or deed or rare counterexample) for me. And Aman, my stepson; how did you get to be so wise at age seventeen, dammit? And while we're on family, a loud shout-out to my brother, Jay, who has taught me more about forgiveness than anyone else, by making it a nonissue. I love you, bro.

And I want to thank Dick Wagner and John Levy. You two were the first ones to say, "Hey, there's a book in these weekly columns of yours." How did you know this by the third column? Your constant support has been heartwarming and, believe me, necessary. And to George Kinder, Cicily Maton, and Michelle Maton, my thanks for wiring me into the financial life planning profession, where I have met dozens and dozens of wonderful people I dare call friends. You have shown me how possible it is, and how life affirming, to bring both an open heart and an acute mind to one's work. I thank all of you.

How could I complete a book with *appreciative* in the title without including an acknowledgement of my teachers of Appreciative Inquiry? David Cooperrider, Diana Whitney, Jane Macgruder Watkins, and Ralph Kelly, you all have brought something vital, priceless, and necessary to the world, and to me.

To Jackie Kelm, for being such a sterling model, cogent writer, and joyful friend, and to Susan Belgard, for lighting the way with such care, delight, and timely wisdom, my deep thanks. Given the miracle of cyber friendships, it will be a blast to meet each of you in person someday.

A deep bow to Buddhist teachers who have shown me a way to wisdom and compassion: Thich Nhat Hanh, (the late) Thay Giac Thanh, Sylvia Boorstein, George Kinder (yes, the same one who introduced me to financial life planners; versatile guy, that George), and Jack Lawlor.

And to Hal Zina Bennett, my friend, writing teacher, and book coach. Who knew how complicated it would be to take a bunch of columns and make a book out of it? Thanks, Hal, for demanding that this book have *bookness*.

And finally, my thanks again to Jody, for being wife, friend, lover, teacher, inspiration, and fellow traveler, and for having the starring role in so many of these chapters. My acknowledgments, and my joys, begin and end with you.

Foreword:
Appreciating Appreciative Moments

If we all did the things we are capable of doing,
we would literally astound ourselves.

—Thomas Alva Edison

This book will teach you how to astound yourself. Not only will Ed Jacobson's thoughtful, funny, and wise writing inspire you to become more than you ever dreamed possible, it will also walk with you on each step of your journey toward that state of *more*. Ed's aim in this book, and in all his work, is to teach us how to see what is life affirming and good in every moment of our "one wild and precious life" (to borrow Mary Oliver's beautiful phrase), to unlock our dreams and create the most inviting future we can imagine. And Ed's aim is excellent! As I read each chapter, I found myself effortlessly whisked away to my inner world, aided by his ideas and his supportive voice suggesting how I might do, be present in, and enjoy my personal and professional life even better, and thereby gain even more joy.

I love this book! The chapters are thirty-four perfect packages, each one complete with profound insights, memorable stories, inspirational quotes, and simple, straightforward exercises for applying it all. They will have the effect of bringing you home to yourself, as Ed would phrase it. You can savor one package a day, in ten or fifteen minutes, or indulge in an entire smorgasbord of appreciation. Either way, your life will never be the same, which might be the understatement of the year.

Take telephone meditation, for example. I'll never pick up the phone in the same way again, and neither will you after reading chapter 20. Thanks to Ed, I now use the time while the phone is ringing to pause and center myself, and set an intention for the ensuing conversation. The phone has taken on a completely new meaning for me. So have staircases; read chapter 21 to see what I mean. These are but two of dozens of simple, practical ways that this book will change your life for the better. But there's more.

Every page feels like a wake-up-call to the heart, to live and love more fully. It is a book you will return to again and again when you want to reconnect with timeless appreciative principles and practices, and reconnect to yourself. By the time you've read through it, you'll feel as if you have a new lease on life, with the motivation and tools to get you moving in the right direction. Wow—it doesn't get much better than that, does it?

Well, actually it does. There's the author himself, Ed. As you turn each page, you get a deeper glimpse into this amazing man. Ed is highly experienced and well-read, but more importantly, he's "well-lived." He clearly walks his talk, and has studied and practiced with an incredible breadth of masters and experts. I have the distinct impression that he remembers and recollects everything he has read, seen, heard, and experienced. His passages are imbued with ideas and quotes from some of the world's most respected teachers, and the book is worth the references alone.

And the best part of all is that Ed will not only make you think, but he will make you *smile*. You will feel his heart, and his wisdom, on every page. His style is so warm and such fun, you'll miss him when the book is over. His writing feels so personal, it's like he's standing next to you, cheering you on. You'll find yourself thinking, "Yeah—I can do this!"

But of course you'll never know until you open up the package. So go ahead—your life is calling. Astound yourself.

—Jacqueline Kelm, author of *Appreciative Living: The Principles of Appreciative Inquiry in Personal Life*

The Journey of Appreciation

Appreciative Moments began two years ago as a weekly column that explored various aspects of living and working from an appreciative, life affirming perspective. At the outset, I compiled a lengthy topic list, based on my passion for two related areas of the social sciences: Appreciative Inquiry (AI), the positive, strength-based approach to personal and organizational change that forms the backbone of this book; and positive psychology, whose philosophy and research fit nicely with AI. I looked forward to exploring those eighty-five topics in the columns and sharing them via e-mail with clients, colleagues, family, and friends. Each column was designed to be read in a minute or two, hence its name "This Appreciative Moment."

The first few columns focused, as intended, on AI's principles and positive psychology's research findings. However, as I began to feather in stories from my personal and professional experience in order to bring the principles and research to life, the response of readers grew, both in enthusiasm and in frequency. Correspondingly, the distribution list began to expand by word of mouth, and now stands at more than six hundred names. People frequently tell me that they forward the columns to others so, given the workings of the Internet, I have no way of knowing just how many receive the columns. My reader correspondents have taught me that my writing has the deepest meaning and impact when I use my own life experiences, and my reflections about them, as the subject matter of the writing. The process of self-reflection continues to drive the content of the columns, as it has driven the writing of this book.

In addition to learning about how my writing contributes to others, I have received a truly profound teaching: the more I write about appreciation as a way of being, and the implications of venturing onto this path, the more I wind up living with greater appreciation and authenticity in my own life. There are two reasons for this phenomenon that bear mention.

The first is that, as a result of my prolonged immersion in the whys and wherefores of appreciative living, it has seeped into my character. You simply can't marinate in this stuff without being transformed by it. My hope and wish for you is that, as you read this book and experiment with the exercises at the end of each chapter, you will experience this marinating process and gradually be transformed.

The second is that cognitive dissonance is at play. Every time I become aware that I am talking the talk about living and working appreciatively (i.e., looking for someone's positive core, focusing on her potential, and centering myself to respond rather than react) without walking the walk, I experience palpable discomfort and tension. My way of closing the agonizing gap between *writing about* my life and *doing* my life is to strive to become the person I write about: kinder, more patient, more forward-looking, more appreciative, more playful, more open to possibility. I would love for this book to move you further in that direction as well.

Like all of us, I'm a work in progress at this business of appreciation. That's why I titled this introduction "The Journey of Appreciation." I arrive at a place of appreciation from time to time, but I never stay there very long. Events (and my often unskillful responses to them) take me out of that appreciative space for a time, until I can lift myself back into it again. This process has taught me another profound lesson: falling down and getting back up is a core part of the journey of appreciation.

Before plunging into the book, a few helpful words: (1) This isn't a book that you need to read from start to finish, according to the order of the chapters. Each is written as a stand-alone reading. So you can open to any page or start by reading what most attracts your attention. (2) You will find exercises at the end of each chapter, intended for readers who like to process new information experientially. These exercises offer a way of bringing key lessons into your everyday life at a practical level. I call them "practices" because each one can be adopted as an ongoing habit, or practice. (3) If you keep a journal, you may find that these exercises offer guidelines for areas to explore and write about. (4) Throughout the country, people are finding it helpful to form small groups to explore the concepts of Appreciative Inquiry and other positively focused approaches. There are also blogs and online chat groups dedicated to this work. For guidelines on starting your own group, see the afterword "Now What?"

Ready to plunge in? I hope you enjoy the water.

Chapter 1:
Welcome to My Life's Work

*A*ppreciative Inquiry is a way of approaching each situation and each person (including oneself) with an appreciative eye and ear, a sense of awe and possibility, and an open heart. When I was introduced to AI in 1997, I knew I'd found a way of working and living that had great meaning and promise for me. In fact, at the end of training, I wrote a note to myself: "If I don't do this work, I won't be true to myself." That much I knew. What I didn't know was that it would become my life's work.

It took me three or four years to integrate Appreciative Inquiry deeply in my work. Since then, appreciation and open inquiry have become the centerpieces not only of my work, but of my entire life as well. This ongoing process is a journey, a continuing delight, and sometimes a daunting challenge. I have written this book as a way to guide you on such a path, to light the way … and perhaps to lighten the way as well.

From Appreciative Inquiry, I have learned that I function best when I'm operating from appreciation and possibility—and with openness to (a) seeing the best in each person, in each situation, in the wider world, and in myself; and to (b) building on that sense of possibility to create the best experiences, learning environments, and tangible outcomes I can. Of course, I'm not always at my best. I don't always operate from possibility and appreciation. That's why it's called practice—because it takes a lot of it. And by practicing appreciation (and getting up again when I've fallen short on it), I've gleaned some valuable insights, which I have incorporated throughout *Appreciative Moments.*

And so I've discovered that my life's work is about bringing appreciation, wonder, and possibility to each individual and group I'm with, and about exploring what that perspective would look like, how it might operate, and the riches it would bring in work and in life. Welcome to my life's work.

Perhaps the best and quickest way to capture the richness and beauty of Appreciative Inquiry is to create short phrases to keep in mind or write on Post-it Notes™. Here are my top five:

- What is this person's positive core? How can we bring it out more?

- What's good here, and how can we get more of it?

- What is positive and life-affirming in this situation? How can we build on this foundation to achieve our goals?

- When are we at our best? How can we be at our best more often?

- What do we deeply wish for? How can we bring our best selves to the process of achieving this shared and heartfelt aspiration?

One of the foundational tools of Appreciative Inquiry is the appreciative question. This type of question is formulated in a positive way, and seeks to uncover and bring out high point experiences, strengths, successes, aspirations, and other positive aspects of one's experience and strivings. For example, "How are you doing?" is not appreciative. "What's been a high point in your day thus far?" is.

I invite you to consider the following appreciative question as a way of finding, or confirming, your own life's work: how often can you say about your job, "Welcome to my life's work"? Trust your immediate response. It contains more than a kernel of truth. For example, perhaps you heard yourself say, "Oh, about ten percent of the time," "Gosh, it's probably ninety percent," "Well, every time I'm with a client, I know I'm welcoming that person to my life's work," or "That question makes me uncomfortable." Any response is fine. Each one reveals something important about your life's work.

A powerful way to use appreciative questions is to inquire about high point experiences. Let's use some follow-up appreciative questions to learn more about such experiences.

Can you remember a time when you found yourself thinking or saying, "Yes! This is the work I was meant to do in the world"? What memory arises in your mind? (If you like, you can write down your answer.) If that question doesn't elicit a memory, consider these two alternative questions:

- Can you remember a time when you felt totally immersed in and excited by your work?

- Can you recall a time when you used your gifts to make a difference—a difference that truly mattered to yourself or to someone else?

For either of those questions, here are some details to consider:

- What was the situation?

- What challenges did you face?

- What gifts did you use?

- Who else was involved, and what did that person do?

- How did you feel in that situation? (Don't gloss over this one. It's centrally important.)

- How did the situation turn out?

- What important lessons did you learn?

- And the most important question to ask:

- What would it take to make this your life's work?

If, after reading this chapter and living with these questions, (a) you feel confirmed in the choices you've made regarding your work life, and/or (b) you're gaining insights about how you could create more experiences of that type for yourself, that's wonderful. Alternatively, if (c) you've become uncomfortable about your answers, you've been paying attention and are equally to be congratulated. Self-awareness is always the first step on our journey to becoming what we might become.

Don't rush away from the discomfort. Live with the question of what has produced it, what it may be telling you, and what your life is asking of you. The answers can guide you to your life's work. Don't rush to find the right answers or to dispel the discomfort or distress you might be feeling. Those difficult emotions may be signs that your life's work is calling to you. You owe it to yourself to listen, and to follow.

Practice

In his book *Callings: Finding and Following an Authentic Life*, Gregg Levoy defines a calling as being one-half of a conversation: a call that demands a response. This chapter presents the following questions to guide you in identifying your life's work. This week, let those questions course through you and call to you:

- How often can I honestly say about the work I do, "Welcome to my life's work"?

- Can I remember a time when I felt totally immersed in and excited by my work?

- Can I recall a time when I used my gifts to make a difference—a difference that mattered to myself or to someone else?

Do your answers reveal something that you are called to do in the world? That you are called to be in the world? If so, take the first step (or the next step) toward it. Journal about it, talk about it with someone you trust, do research about it in books and magazines, interview someone who's following a similar calling, or take another step that will move you forward. After that, let the next step reveal itself to you. Trust the process.

Chapter 2:
How Was Your Day?

*H*ow often do you ask questions such as, "How was your day?" "How was your Memorial Day weekend?" or the bane of school-age children all over the planet: "What did you learn today?" And how often has a family member, friend, or co-worker asked you this type of question? Mind you, there's nothing wrong with this type of question. It's usually asked with genuinely good intentions, although maybe a little mechanically. So, let's do a radical and appreciative makeover on these questions: our very own reality TV show. Let's call it *You're Asking That?!*

Instead of asking how someone's day was, say, "Tell me about one thing that brightened your day today." Or ask, "What did you especially enjoy today?" And instead of asking how someone's holiday was, try asking, "What was a highlight of your holiday?"

When you read these questions, how did they grab you? What happens when you imagine someone asking them to you, and when you imagine yourself asking them to a family member, friend, or colleague? When I envision myself being on the receiving end of these questions, I get a jolt of positive energy, and I think to myself, "Wow! This person is actually interested in what I experienced." I don't always get that feeling when I'm asked, "How was your day?" or, "How was the weekend?" Usually, I answer, "Fine," and then move on without feeling much connection with the person.

You can ask these types of question at any moment. You needn't reserve them for the daily retrospective. Ask a colleague, a client, or a family member phoning to check in, "What's been the best part of your day so far?" I love asking this question, for many reasons.

First, it can perk up people. Simply by asking them to recall and verbalize high point moments, I'm triggering the same parts of their brains that were stimulated when they had the original experiences about which I'm asking. This automatically puts them in a better mood. More good news: we can also do this for ourselves, thereby giving ourselves a mini-jolt that takes less than a minute and keeps us going. It's less expensive, and lower in calories and caffeine, than a Starbucks beverage and a sweet roll.

Second, I perk up from knowing that someone I care about has been enriched by something positive that happened this very day. It makes me feel good.

Third, it gets the conversation going in a lively and positive direction. I'm all in favor of virtuous cycles: those one-positive-thing-leads-to-another-positive-thing deals. They're so much more life enhancing than an endless round of "You'll never guess what!" Admittedly, office gossip often feels delicious, and it makes for bonding between the mutually aggrieved. But it's no more nourishing than a sugar high. It doesn't last, and it leads to a nasty crash. This is a classic vicious cycle of gossip and crash. I'm not in favor of vicious cycles, and you shouldn't be either. They aren't good for you.

Fourth, it can fortify the two of us for the conversation that we're there to have. This brief and positive check-in can create just the boost that each of us might need for dealing with the heavier agenda items to follow. I like to think of it as a glide path into the tough stuff. Even if we both know that we're consciously conspiring to share positive stories in order to elevate ourselves for a challenging task, we also know that it's among the most benign of social conspiracies, and it's performed for good reason: it works.

Fifth, and last, it can teach us to enrich ourselves and each other in the future by using such questions for frequent mini-boosts. This is especially valuable when other parts of our days haven't gone so well. Psychologists call this practice self-soothing, and it's one of the healthiest things we can do for ourselves. It doesn't mean we're denying the heavier, darker stuff. It does mean that we're making a conscious choice between alternative ways of dealing with the day, and we recognize that our choices will determine how the next portion of the day goes. That strikes me as a real crossroads. Choosing the positive fork is the healthy, mature choice. Not always the easy choice, but always healthy.

Maybe fifth and last wasn't last, after all. If you adopt the practice of using such questions with yourself, you're also likely to practice doing so with others, thus passing it along the great chain of being. Maybe there is no last reason at all.

Try it on for size. You might find that the time you spend sharing this type of question and listening to the answers it generates becomes the best part of your day!

Practice

This week, instead of your tried-and-true greetings, be on the lookout for opportunities to ask questions like the following:

- What's been a highlight of your day thus far?

- What's brightened your day thus far?

- What's making you happy today?

- What are you looking forward to the most this weekend?

- What was a high point of your weekend (or holiday)?

Make a mental note of how people respond, how you feel asking the questions and hearing their responses, and how the ensuing conversations go. Pay attention to comments they make about the uniqueness of the questions. Try varying the questions and improvising your own. In time, you'll develop your own style for asking these questions that will feel right for you. Above all, have fun with them. See how your day goes.

Chapter 3:
Letting Our Souls
Catch up with Us

The story is told of a South American tribe that went on a long march. Day after day they traveled. Then, all of a sudden, they would stop walking and sit down to rest. They'd make camp and stay in one place for a couple of days before going any further. They explained that they did this because they needed this time of rest so that their souls could catch up with them.

—from *Sabbath,* by Wayne Muller

I love this passage. I tell it often to emphasize how critical it is that we remember to let our souls catch up with us. I'm using the story here to introduce a practice that I call the two-minute drill, designed to take place between meetings, other significant activities in our workdays, or any activities in our overscheduled lives. The purpose of the drill is to bring you back to your center and prepare you to bring your entire self to the next activity. It's a great way of letting your soul catch up with you.

What you decide to include in your two-minute drill depends entirely on what works for you—what brings you back to a calm, centered, and balanced state. You may find that closing your eyes and taking five or ten slow, deep breaths is an essential part of your drill. Or you may enjoy doing a simple breath meditation—by closing your eyes and paying attention to your breath (however shallow or deep), from the in-breath through to the out-breath—for five or ten repetitions. Some people find yoga postures or stretching exercises helpful. None of these activities need to take more than one or two minutes, and they can all be valuable in restoring and replenishing you.

To create a welcoming environment for the next person or activity, you'll also want to clear your physical environment (be it your desk at work, your kitchen table, or another venue) of anything that smacks of clutter. Of course, it's also essential that you rebalance your internal environment. Your clients, your associates, and your family deserve and need to have all of you there. So do you.

Some people find that they need more than two minutes for their drill. Some take as long as fifteen minutes, using this time to complete their notes, reflect on the recently concluded conversation, and meditate before their next appointment. My former therapist burned a cedar stick in his office between appointments to clear the air of the previous conversation and return it, and him, to center. I often marveled at how this practice (which he referred to as "smudging the space") seemed to contribute to his equanimity, and at the discipline that it seemed to require. And at how lovely it was to catch the faint, fading fragrance of cedar as I approached his office. It was a pleasant way of beckoning me to enter … and find wholeness.

My own two-minute drill for coaching conversations takes about ten minutes. Typically, I'm working in my upstairs office (my real office) until fifteen minutes prior to the appointment time. Here's my ritual: I put aside what I'm doing, place my desktop computer on standby, take several slow and mindful breaths, neaten up my desk, and take my client file (which I'd already placed at the ready) downstairs to the living room.

Once there, I arrange the table where I sit for coaching appointments so that it's just right: telephone, client file, blank paper, pen, clock, water glass ... and nothing else. I read through my notes of the most recent conversation and do a few minutes of calming breath meditation while awaiting the call. I then spend a couple of minutes conjuring up a glistening visual image of this person, my coaching client, at his best. I find that having in mind that unfailingly positive image of this unique individual puts me in a wonderful place of welcoming—a state of positive anticipation—so that when the phone rings, I find myself automatically smiling at the gift that awaits me. (I know that sounds sappy, but it's true. Try it yourself, and see if it doesn't work that way.) The ten minutes devoted to this ritual are a great investment in letting my soul catch up with me. This is vital if I am to help people let their souls catch up with them.

What is your version of the two-minute drill? How long does it take you, and when is the last time you did it? If this is a new concept for you, experiment with it and create your own version. Find out what works best for you. You'll want to tell your colleagues or family about what you're doing, so they can support your need for privacy, silence, or whatever else your drill requires. (By the way, they will likely be fascinated, and they may well create their own unique versions.)

Whatever form your two-minute drill takes, you'll find that at the end of the workday, you're much more refreshed and vital. And that your soul has been right there with you, all day long.

Practice

If you have a favorite two-minute drill, plan to use it this week between appointments or tasks on your to-do list. If you don't have a two-minute drill, you can create one by adopting some of the following three ideas from this chapter (or improvise your own):

- Close your eyes and take between five and ten slow, deep breaths.

- Do a simple breath-centered meditation: close your eyes and follow your breathing, without controlling how shallow or deep it is, through five or ten repetitions.

- Do yoga postures that you enjoy, and that relax and center you.

Whether you already have such a drill or not, here are a couple of pointers:

1. When it comes time to do your drill, resist the temptation to do it later. The impulse to postpone it probably means that you need the respite now. Just do it.

2. Give yourself at least three consecutive days of practicing this form of self-soothing and centering. Note its effects on your energy, your mood, and your productivity. See if your soul has caught up with you.

Chapter 4:
How Full Is Your Bucket?

*M*y wife and I attended a high school graduation party yesterday. While there, I spied a young man whom I remembered as having acted in the high school's recent production of *Fiddler on the Roof.* I went up to him and said, "I saw you in *Fiddler* recently, didn't I? I almost didn't recognize you without your beard." He smiled at being remembered, and I then told him how much I had enjoyed his performance—all three performances, in fact. (My stepson had a small role in the play, so we took in as many performances as we could.) He absolutely beamed! Turning to a friend, he said, "Hey, he just made my day!" I was surprised at his exclamation because he looked like he was already having a rather good day.

I recently read a wonderful little book titled *How Full Is Your Bucket? Positive Strategies for Work and Life,* by Tom Rath and his grandfather, the late Donald Clifton, PhD. (Clifton is known as both the father of strengths psychology and the grandfather of positive psychology.) The book's theme is that each of us is equipped with a bucket (in which our supply of positive emotions is stored) and a dipper (which we use to fill or deplete other people's buckets). All of us know life-affirming people who always seem to fill others' buckets with praise, smiles, acts of generosity, and speaking well of others. Sadly, we also know people who deplete others' storehouses of positive emotions. Such folks are sometimes called toxic, sourpusses, or downers. They're also known by other names, most of which are not uttered in polite company.

The authors cite research showing that full buckets are associated with many positive outcomes: greater happiness, closer relationships, higher productivity, and creativity, decisions that are more effective, lower stress, and greater resilience (i.e., ability to rebound from adversity). And here's some amazing news. There's even strong evidence that positive emotions lead to better health and longer life! Don't we want all those outcomes for our clients, work associates friends, families, and ourselves? In our more generous moments, don't we want those outcomes for everyone? Think about it this way. It costs nothing to fill someone's bucket, and it leads to such well-being for both others and ourselves. If you're inclined to economic analysis, the benefit-cost ratio is infinite. Such a deal!

The bucket-and-dipper model provides a vivid visual image that we can use as we go about our lives, to help us enrich others and enrich ourselves. The research also shows that enriching others and enriching ourselves is mutually reinforcing. If we fill others' buckets, we find ourselves enriched and enhanced because we have set in motion a virtuous cycle of positivity. It's a wonderful case of what goes around comes around.

Yesterday's interaction with that young actor perfectly illustrated a virtuous cycle. His reaction told me I had filled his bucket, and his response telling me I had just made his day, pretty much made mine.

Sadly, the converse is also true: if we disparage, deplete, or diminish others, we are not only dipping from their buckets but from our own as well. All of us know sourpusses who delight in others' misery. And in our own sour moods, we can have that same bucket diminishing effect. It always sets vicious cycles in motion.

We can use our dippers to increase others' buckets (and thereby fill our own), or we can use it to reduce others' (and our own) happiness and future resilience. The authors' bucket-and-dipper metaphor is a vivid and compelling image, and their admonition, "The choice is ours, in each moment," is a powerful reminder to choose the higher moral ground. I use their words to guide me in speaking helpfully, acting generously, and refraining from sour words and acts. I'm not always able to catch myself, but I'm getting better at it, guided by the mental image of my bucket and dipper. It's amazing what a little self-restraint can do to free up the better angels of our nature.

How full is your bucket? And how can you fill it by filling others' buckets?

Practice

1. This week, be aware of each time you fill others' buckets and each time you dip from theirs. Observe what happens as a result of each type of action.

2. Be aware each time you experience someone filling your bucket through kind words, actions, or gestures. Note your own reactions to receiving such acts. Similarly, observe when others dip from your bucket by using unskillful words, actions, or nonverbal gestures. Note your reactions.

3. Pay attention to bucket-filling and bucket-depleting behavior that you observe directed toward others, and observe how those situations turn out. Also, note your own internal response to what you are witnessing.

4. See if reading this chapter and adopting the above three practices has changed your feelings and reactions toward bucket-filling and bucket-depleting—whether done by you or others.

Chapter 5:
Discovery

*W*hile preparing for a couple of upcoming presentations recently, my mind got busy creating a few appreciative questions on which participants could reflect. I soon realized that while these questions might not work in the presentations, they'd make a dandy focus for a piece on *discovery*. Let me explain.

Discovery is the first stage of an Appreciative Inquiry process. In this phase, pairs of people interview each other on an affirmative topic. (A classic AI affirmative topic is "a time of excitement, engagement, and involvement in your work.") I love the term discovery. It conveys the sense of innocent childlike wonder much more than the term *data collection* does. Thinking of discovering the essence of a person through listening to his story opens us to the riches of the story, and it helps us relax our critical, judgmental faculty.

Yet we don't need to attend a workshop or be interviewed in order to discover something important about ourselves. We can discover ourselves in other ways. Most forms of meditation, for example, involve a silent, inward focus. Many wonderful books invite readers to reflect on wise sayings, quotations, and questions posed for their benefit. This chapter is squarely in that tradition. The following three topics provide self-directed practices that you can use for personal discovery.

I invite you to sit back in a relaxed position, center yourself by taking several slow, deep breaths, and run your eyes over the following three sets of questions. Spend some time with one, two, or all three, and see where each one takes you. Feel free to share the questions with anyone you think would enjoy and profit from reflecting on them. Give these folks the gift of *discovery*.

1. Being at Your Best

When are you at your best as a person? Can you think of a specific time when the way you were acting, feeling, and thinking was you at your very best? As you think of such a time, here are some questions to ask yourself:

- What were the circumstances?

- What were you were doing, feeling, thinking?

- How did others respond to what you did?

- What feelings and sensations are you now experiencing as you recall that time?

- How can you be you at your best more of the time? What would it require from you? What role might others play? What would be your very first step? (Plan to take that step at the next opportunity.)

If no specific event comes to mind, complete this sentence: "I'm always at my best when...." If you can identify circumstances that typically bring out your best, perhaps you can then think of a specific time when those circumstances worked their magic especially well and brought out your best. If not, that's perfectly okay. Simply go on to the next question. You can always come back to this one.

You may well find that a story occurs to you sometime later, without consciously thinking about it.

2. Feeling Connected with Another Person

Think of someone important to you, perhaps your spouse, partner, child, parent, good friend, or someone else. Fix the person's image vividly in your mind's eye. When do you feel most connected with this person? Does a specific time come to mind, a time when you felt especially close to and connected with him? If so, recall this time as vividly as you can (closing your eyes will help).

- What was the setting?

- What led up to that time of feeling so connected?

- What were you doing at the time?

- How did you experience feeling connected? Where did you feel it in your body? What thoughts went through your mind?

The sense of feeling connected comes and goes. It's not a one-time event or a twenty-four-seven phenomenon, which leads to the next questions:

- What can you do to feel more deeply connected, and connected more often, to this person? Would those same practices work to help you feel more connected with others?

3. Doing What You Just Love to Do

Think of an activity you simply love doing. It could be a work activity, a sport or hobby, an activity with family or friends … anything at all. It might be something you feel immersed and in flow while doing; perhaps time races by as you're engaged in it. In your mind's eye, see if you can fix a vivid image of yourself doing this activity. Also, tune into the bodily experience of how you feel when you're immersed in it. If you can recall a specific time, so much the better.

- What aspects of the activity, the setting, or others who were present contributed to your experience?

- What sensations and feelings do you experience as you recollect it?

- Are you satisfied with how frequently you have this experience? If so, that's great. If not, what could you do to engage in that activity more of the time?

- Now, let's think about it in another way: what could you do to create that level of passion and flow in your other activities?

I find questions such as those above to be like Altoid Peppermints™: they're curiously strong. They demonstrate the power of appreciatively phrased questions to be wonderful companions on our path of self-discovery.

Practice

1. Ask yourself each of the three sets of discovery questions presented above, about the following topics:

    - Being your best
    - Feeling connected with another person
    - Doing what you love to do

    Do each set of questions at a different time, allowing time to reflect on and perhaps write down your answers. See what you discover about yourself and about the power of discovery questions of this type.

2. Once you have completed these sets of questions, ask one or more of them with someone you know well. Explain in advance that you have worked with the questions yourself and have benefited from them, and that you would like to offer the person that same opportunity. Allow a half hour for each set of questions, to ensure plenty of time for reflection and discussion. Depending on the person's level of interest, consider asking two or all three sets. Debrief him at the end, asking one simple question: "How was that for you?"

Chapter 6:
Refrigerator Magnet Thinking

*I*n thinking about Appreciative Inquiry, I find it useful to reduce its core to simple expressions—the kind that could fit on a refrigerator magnet. Recall Kevin Costner playing the role of journeyman catcher Crash Davis in the screwball comedy *Bull Durham*. Fed up with the loopy antics of his pitcher, Nuke LaLoosh (memorably played by Tim Robbins), Crash holds a conference with him on the mound, quickly and tersely getting to the heart of the matter. "Look," he says, "baseball is a simple game." (World-weary pause.) "You throw the ball." (Pause again.) "You hit the ball." (Pause yet again.) "You catch the ball." End of conference.

If it can be done with something as rich and layered as baseball, surely we can express the richness and layering of Appreciative Inquiry with a few vivid phrases. This chapter introduces one particular refrigerator magnet maxim of AI. Distilled to its essence, Appreciative Inquiry asks the following:

What's good here—and how can we get more of it?

When I think of that question, I envision a Columbo-type character (wrinkled raincoat and all) engaging in a relentless quest for the positive, life-affirming aspects of a person, a family, a work group, a situation ... or whatever. It's a quest not only to locate those qualities, but to magnify them until they capture the attention of everyone he alerts to them, as though shouting, "Hey, you! Pay attention! This is good stuff!" And then our Columbo asks the profoundly simple question "What would it take for us to have more of that?"

It cuts through complexity and confusion, doesn't it? And through the yes-but-you-don't-understands, as well as through our myriad other ways of making ourselves into victims and keeping ourselves stuck.

There's a name for those who do this work of cutting through to the good stuff, to the gems. No, it's not Pollyanna, and it's not Mary Poppins. Those two characters are denying the "other" stuff. The Columbo people I'm referring to don't deny the ills, the deficiencies, the injustices, the dark side. Instead, they choose to focus their energies, attention, and efforts on finding and embracing the good, life-giving stuff. In fact, the term used by researchers who have found such individuals is *good-finders*. It may come as no surprise to learn that these Columbos-of-the-Positive tend to lead longer, more vigorous, more fulfilled, and more successful lives.

When I strive to serve as a good-finder in organizations that I enter as a consultant or participant, I make a conscious effort to focus on what (and who) is life-affirming there and to put aside my well-honed critical eye and ear. When I'm making a presentation in front of twenty (or five hundred and twenty) people, I can become overly focused on someone who's fidgeting in the front row, and begin to think scary thoughts such as, "Oh no! I'm losing the crowd!" Then I stop that unhelpful self-talk and tell myself what the truth is: I'm in front of twenty (or five hundred and twenty) friends that I haven't met yet, and I have a wonderful gift to share with them. And in my family I need to be aware of how easily I can let myself feel provoked, almost always over a trifle or an imagined slight, and to remind myself of how much I am loved, and what wonderful people they are.

What would it take for you to become a full-time good-finder? It takes at least these three things for me to aspire to that calling:

- The **faith** (call it appreciative faith) that good-finding is a reliable path to greater effectiveness, productivity, gratification, and happiness—my own and others'. This faith sustains me when I'm in a situation fraught with negativity, conflict, or peril. I sometimes recall that sunny optimist Ronald Reagan, whose favorite expression was, "With all this horse manure, there must be a pony here somewhere." At such times, I remember that my job is to find that pony. And when I open wide my appreciative eyes and ears, I'm stunned at how much good stuff I find. This continuous discovery always strengthens my appreciative faith in being a good-finder.

- A **willingness** to lay down my weapons of mass negativity; to let go of faultfinding, blaming, searching for the perpetrator; and most of all, to stop spinning stories that feature me in the role of victim-in-chief. These stories usually begin with, "This just isn't right!" (Decades of professional experience have taught me that I am not unique in possessing this negativity, which is somewhat comforting.) I've started to get rather good at seeing those inner monologues as simply being storylines in my fictional melodrama. That awareness gives me the time and space I need to regain my perspective, to take myself less seriously, and to strengthen my faith in this good-finding business.

- **Practice! Practice! Practice!** After all, that's how you get to Carnegie Hall. It takes putting on my Nikes and just doing it. And here's something important I've learned. The more I look for the good stuff and make a big deal about it, the more self-reinforcing it becomes. After practicing it for a while, I've developed a real taste for it, and I can no longer tolerate dour folks who diminish the life around them. My friend Helen calls them energy vampires.

You might be asking yourself, "Why does he bother? What's in it for him?"

- For one thing, I do it because it works. I feel lighter, more joyful, and more playful in situations where I can be a good-finder. I wonder if you've ever stopped to ponder what hard work (not to mention soul-crushing work) it is to be on the alert for faults, deficits, mistakes, weaknesses, and other so-called defects continually. Believe me, I know how hard and debilitating it can be. I did it for fifteen years as a well-paid corporate consultant, and for years before that as a psychology professor and psychotherapist. In addition to being hard work, it doesn't do the job. And I'll tell you one more thing: it's hard to quit doing it cold turkey, but it's a rewarding path of recovery … and discovery.

- I get to appreciate the positive qualities of the people I'm with and the situation I'm in. What's more, people I'm with tell me they feel better, lighter, and more joyful because I've brought my loving spotlight with me, and I'm shining it on them. And in those situations, all of us learn valuable things we wouldn't have discovered otherwise: (a) where the good stuff is, and what it looks like; (b) how to have that good stuff more of the time (the surprising reality: it's not that difficult to do); and (c) how to be better good-finders. That's a tri-fecta, if ever there was one.

That's what it takes: appreciative faith, lying down my sword of judgment, and lots of practice. And I reap those riches in return.

I wonder if you have an underdeveloped good-finder within you. Did you decide, like so many of us, to "Stop that foolishness!" when you were eleven or twelve because it wasn't considered cool by your peers to be cheerfully enthusiastic? If so, welcome back. Can you imagine becoming more of a full-time good-finder, and doing it full-heartedly, as though your life and the lives and welfare of those who count on you depended on it? They might, you know.

Practice

1. Give your well-honed critical faculty the gift of a one-day sabbatical. In its place, focus your attention on being a goodfinder: discover what's useful, beautiful, insightful, and/or moving in your meetings, your conversations, your reading, and other activities for that one day. Be on the lookout for the strengths and virtues in people, ideas, and situations. Imagine you're on a scavenger hunt. See how many you can bring back.

    You may find that this hunt for the positive feels unnatural and awkward. For each positive you discover, you may find yourself reflexively pushing back with responses of the "Yes, but ..." variety. I find that the best antidote to this reflex is to allow it to express its opinion, respond to it with a polite, "Thank you for sharing." and return to your search for positives. ("Thank you for sharing" does two things. It acknowledges that there's an inner voice seeking to be heard, and it robs that voice of its customary sting. Try it. Find out how it works for you.)

    See what you learn, what you discover, and how you like this good-finding business. Ask yourself, "What's good about good-finding, and how can I do more of it?"

2. Decide whether to extend the one-day critical faculty sabbatical for one more day.

3. After doing practices 1 and 2 for a while, consider declaring each Tuesday (or another day) your good-finding day. See if it spreads to other days.

4. Create one or more refrigerator magnet expressions that inspire, motivate, and/or energize you. Select one and put its message into effect for one day. (You might write it on a sticky note or an index card, or make it your computer's screensaver, to keep the expression front and center.) See what happens.

Chapter 7:
What Would Your
Favorite Hero Do?

*A*ll of us have times when we're simply stumped about how to how to handle a situation: a dead-ended conversation that's been chilled by a stony or embarrassing silence, a difference in viewpoints, or a discussion going in a direction we're uncomfortable with. I've encountered these types of situation any number of times, and I imagine you have too. An approach I find useful is to pause, sit back, and ask myself, "What would one of my heroes do in this situation? How would that person handle it?"

The person who comes to my mind at such times may be a religious figure (e.g., Jesus, Buddha, Moses, Mohammed, and so on), a family member or friend, a professional associate, a revered teacher, or a fictional character. The possibilities are endless. At various times, for example, I've found myself substituting Buddha, Jody (my wife), or Ruth.

Most of you don't know who Ruth is ... or, sadly, was. Ruth was the wisest and most brilliant person I've ever known, and she was my most transformative mentor. I first met her when she supervised my work as a postdoctoral field placement student in the Washtenaw County Community Mental Health Center (the CMHC, as we called it). We quickly became soul friends as well as colleagues, and we were able to preserve and deepen our relationship when I became her nominal supervisor in the CMHC agency when my postdoctoral year ended in 1974. For many of us in Ann Arbor, back in the 1970s and 1980s, she was the star of our internal production of the long-running hit *What Would Ruth Do?*

It's some sixteen years since she passed on, and I've never stopped missing her. She still occasionally guest stars in my dreams. Each time, she's come back to life, and all of us are crazy with delight, like when Michael Jordan came to his senses and realized he'd never be more than a journeyman as a baseballer, gave up his quest to become the Michael Jordan of baseball, and returned triumphantly, like Napoleon from Elba, to the Chicago Bulls. I was living in Chicago at the time, and I'll tell you this: the town went absolutely bonkers!

In the dream, with Ruth back among us, I always ask her a question, and she always responds. But I can never make out her words. They always fade like an Etch A Sketch drawing before I can decipher them. It's quite maddening, as you can imagine. I suppose I'm growing up, though. I have the dream less frequently now, and these days I ask myself, "What would I do in this situation, if I were my best self right now?" I no longer rely on Ruth for the answer. Maybe I've simply memorized all her answers, maybe I've truly internalized her wisdom, or maybe I've found my own.

I wonder if you have someone like Ruth in your life, i.e., a person whose wisdom and good sense you have come to rely on, either in real time or in your imagination. Here's how to find out. Think of a vexing situation you're confronting. Call it to mind and ask yourself what your favorite hero would do. See whose name arises to meet your question. The beauty of this approach is that you don't have to prepare in advance. If you trust your instincts, you'll find that the name and image of the powerful role model who's appropriate in that situation will pop up to greet you. Just allow yourself to visualize or listen to how that esteemed model would proceed. Relax, sit back, and enjoy the show. The odds are good that you'll have a vivid image of what to do to break the impasse you're experiencing.

You may be thinking, "Well, I'm simply not that person, so asking myself that question won't do me a bit of good. He could do it. I can't!" However, if you try it, you may be pleasantly surprised by what you find. A good deal of psychology research supports the notion that a vivid image, including an image of someone else handling a situation effectively, can be a powerful guide to our own effective handling of that very situation. Don't be concerned that you won't do it exactly as your heroic role model would, or as well.

The act of asking yourself what your role model would do, and then waiting for the answer to arise within you, has two important effects:

- It reduces the tension that may exist in the room (if you're asking yourself the question while you're physically in the situation).

- It frees up your own creative energies, to guide you in addressing your dilemma.

In fact, research in positive psychology shows that positive emotions, such as feelings of calm or joy, increase the number of options and alternatives we can create for constructive action. Think of it as angioplasty for the mind, blasting through the confusion and the logjam, and allowing us to select a more creative and effective course of action.

When I'm stumped about how to handle a potential conflict situation with my stepson, for example, I don't have to summon up a spiritual figure or a mythic hero. I just ask myself, "How would Jody handle this situation?" Granted, this mother-son duo has a close and unique relationship, and I can't simply mimic her behavior. I would look ridiculous. Besides, Aman would see through it in a heartbeat.

What I can do is visualize what his mother would be doing in such a situation, and then do it in my own way when I'm with him. I can breathe, calm my body, lower my voice, and play for time while I mobilize my best thinking. I try to relate to Aman more like a respectful colleague than a potential adversary. And I try to summon up feelings of love and patience, if I can, and let those feelings guide me.

Truth-in-disclosure time: if I'm simply stumped as to what to do in a sensitive situation with Aman, and if Jody's around and available, I go directly to my oracle of parenting skills and seek her guidance as to how to handle the situation. Someday I'll graduate from needing her expert coaching regarding being a better stepfather. Until that day, I'll continue to use her as an imagined role model when she's not around, asking myself, "What would Jody do?" And when she's available, I'll use her as a coach, by asking her directly for the answer.

Practice

1. Think about your most powerful role models when it comes to behaving effectively in challenging situations. Make a list of their names. For each one, write what it is about the person that makes him a powerful model for you. (In compiling your list, consider that your models may include people you have known, public figures, and characters from literature, movies, theater … and even cartoons.)

2. Now, recall a recent situation that you think you could have handled better. Select two or three of your role models. For

each one, ask yourself, "What would this person have done?" Listen for what they collectively teach you.

3. The next time you are in a dicey situation, mentally review your list of names and see which one pops up to instruct you. Consider following the person's example.

Chapter 8:
Who Are You
When You're at Your Best?

*T*he question that forms the title of this chapter is a hard-core appreciative question. It goes to the heart of living and working appreciatively, and to the heart of our shared human aspiration. There was an expression going around the school when I was an MBA student at Wharton in the early 1980s: he who has the most toys when he dies, wins. Scary, isn't it? Even scarier, I thought it was funny at the time! But more than the desire to accumulate toys in this lifetime, we humans share an aspiration to make the most of the endowment and experience we are given. Mother Teresa captured this sentiment when she instructed her nuns to "let them use you up."

Who are you when you are at your best? This is a great question to use in our workplaces, in our personal relationships, and in our private, reflective moments. Here's how, and why:

- Employers and managers could regularly ask themselves who they are when they are at their best, and they could ask the same question of the members of their organization.

- A work group or team could ask, "When are we at our very best as a team? What are we doing at those times? How are we communicating? How are we treating each other and treating others outside our circle when we're at our best?" And when they have their answers, they can pose the logical follow-up appreciative question, "How can we be those ways, and do those things, more of the time?" If you use these questions with your associates, you'll find that you'll open up your collective minds, your communications, and your self-concept (as individuals and a group), and you'll broaden your ideas about how to become the best organization you can be.

- You can also ask this question of a client—someone you're working with in a coaching, counseling, financial planning, or other service relationship. "Who are you when you're at your best?" makes an excellent lead-in to the process of co-developing a vision of the client's life fully lived, en route to developing a plan of action based on that vision. I can almost guarantee that if you ask your client, "Who are you when you're at your best?" it will be the first time anyone's ever asked him that question.

- In your personal life, you can pose these kinds of questions to family members and friends, about themselves or about the relationship that you have with them. Additionally, asking "Who are we when we're at our best as a family (or as friends)?" is a powerful invitation to deep communication.

If the person isn't able to answer that question straight away, you can help by being more specific: "Tell me a story of a time when you felt as though you were doing exactly what you were meant to be doing, or being the person you always wanted to be. Tell me about the situation, what you were doing, how it felt." And follow up with this question: "How can we arrange conditions so that you can do those things more of the time?" Asking these questions and listening attentively provides the gift of enrichment to the person. It will also enrich you and get the two of you moving toward the shared goal of creating an inspiring vision of the most fulfilling life.

I've used this question and its follow-ups any number of times, at work as well as with family and friends, and always with valuable results. However, my special fondness for it dates from the first time I used it. It was the centerpiece of a session I gave at the end of a Weekend of Possibilities that my friend Roger Breisch convened in late March 2000 at a retreat center in Crystal Lake, Illinois. Roger had invited his friends to gather for an unstructured weekend of connection, conversation, and hilarity. Little did I know that his invitation would change the course of my life, rather dramatically and definitively. Almost all twenty of the weekend's attendees came to the session that I offered on Sunday morning, just before the getaway lunch that brought the weekend to a raucous and pleasing close.

What gives the memory of the session its burnished glow is not the appreciative question itself. Here's the whole story. I was fairly sure, and very hopeful, that the session would attract a tall, good-looking, intelligent, and authentic woman named Jody. I'd felt an instant attraction, and had specifically invited her to my two early morning meditation sessions, both of which she somehow declined to attend. I figured that she would attend this final session along with her friend Marilyn, and would get to see me strut my stuff. I'm happy to report that I was successful: the two of them attended the session, and they appeared to get a great deal from it.

During the Sunday lunch, I had reserved an adjacent seat for her and craftily engineered it so she was sitting next to me. ("Sorry, Jody's sitting here," I said to a procession of people looking for a seat.) She and I made inconsequential small talk during the meal, but at the farewell hug-a-thon, I hugged her good: I used my ten-second special. She revealed much later that this first hug had done the trick. I'd had her from good-bye! A breathless six weeks after that monster hug, I proposed to her. She accepted, approximately 3.15 seconds after I popped the ultimate appreciative question, and the rest, as they say, is history (or destiny). The moral of the story is simply this: it's good to use appreciative questions. (I sometimes think there's a second moral: if you want to get a woman to pay attention to you, you may have to marry her. Don't laugh. It worked for me.)

It's a rather straightforward process: ask a compelling appreciative question and then listen raptly to the answers that arise. I trust this process of asking and listening, and I trust our innate wisdom and experience to provide useful and insightful answers. We don't have to do the laborious, debilitating work of analyzing and dismantling the negative conditions that keep us from being at our best. We don't have to affix blame, criticize, find fault, or play *Gotcha!* with ourselves or someone else. What we need to do is to (a) focus on our highest and best moments, and then (b) create conditions (both inner and outer) that support us in our quests to have more of those moments. This usually means focusing on our own strengths and those of others, rather than on shoring up our weaknesses or theirs.

That's what I did. I asked myself, "Who am I when I am at my very best?" The answer was instantaneous, straightforward, and clear: "Marry the woman!" Again, don't laugh. It worked for me.

Practice

1. Ponder this question: who are you when you are at your very best? (You may want to close your eyes and let the question work its magic with you.)

   After a while, you can open your eyes and answer these follow-up questions:

- How would you describe yourself and what you're doing when you are really the person you were meant to be?

- How would others describe you at such times?

- How do you like this person?

- What would it take for you to be that person more of the time?

- What would it do for you to be that person more often? What would it do for others? For the world?

2. If you find that it's too big a topic to do justice to right now, make an appointment with yourself for later this week to spend some time with it. As the poet Rilke wrote, in *Letters to a Young Poet*, "Live the questions now. Perhaps then, someday far in the future, you will gradually, without even noticing it, live your way into the answer." Let the questions and let the process of inquiry work you. See where they take you.

3. Imagine that it's five years from now, and you are the person you described in either of the first two practices in this chapter. Imagine that you are doing what you were meant to be doing, and being the person you were meant to be, in a complete and full-fledged way.

   - Describe your ideal imagined life, five years from now:

   What does a typical day in your life look like?

   What does a typical week look like, five years from now?

   - Now imagine the steps you took to get to the point of living in accordance with the person you were meant to be, doing what you were meant to do. Describe those steps.

What actions can you take to initiate that journey (or the next step in the journey that you are on) … the one will lead you to that ideal imagined life? Be as specific as you can, as to who can be of help, and what other resources (information, time, money, and so on) you will need.

Chapter 9:
A Happy Memory from Childhood

I always begin a new coaching relationship with a wide-ranging appreciative interview, covering topics from childhood to the present. I learn an incredible amount about the person in this conversation, and we often refer back to this information throughout the coaching journey. The conversation begins with a simple appreciative question: "Can you tell me about a happy memory from your childhood?" It's a wonderful way to initiate myself into this person's life, and a pleasing way for him to guide me there.

My client's answer always tells me something indelibly important about him. It may reveal his fun-loving, gleeful side: remembering skating across the porch of the family home, wearing new skates. Other times, it may reveal an exploratory, solitary side: exploring, by himself, the creeks and woods near a vacation cottage. Or a vigorous, athletic, social personality: recalling summers by the ocean, surrounded by other teens. Whatever the story is, it helps me to form a vivid, positive picture of this person, and what makes him happy. This is important for several reasons:

- It's essential for me to form that unwavering, positive image of this person if I am to coach effectively. (And I believe you must form this same kind of image if you are to effectively serve others, whether clients, customers, parishioners, family members, or anyone else). I can remember every happy memory from childhood story that my coaching clients have told me—even if I can't tell you what I had for breakfast this morning. I carry the resulting positive image of each person with me throughout the coaching relationship. It's always an important part of who people are, and what brings them happiness. Granted, it's not the only part. It is, however, an indispensable part of each one's positive core, and it's important for me to know and value it.

- It lifts the person up at the beginning of an uncertain journey, and it communicates that I'm interested in the client's happiness and in getting to know him. This fortifies him for the road ahead, a road that is likely to contain some bumps and difficult turns.

- If I can access my picture of that happy child at times when all I can see before me is an uncertain, anxious, or confused adult, I can keep the faith for the person—the faith that the journey will lead him back to his home base. In turn, my faith gives the client the courage to traverse whatever difficult times he may confront.

Perhaps you use questions such as "Can you tell me about a happy memory from your childhood?" to initiate your relationships. If you don't, I hope you'll consider experimenting with this question or with one like it. It's not so much the question itself that is important. What is important is that you begin your client relationships in a way that (a) helps you develop an unwavering positive image of your client from the outset, (b) creates positive feelings such as buoyancy or joy in this client at the very start, and (c) enables you to recall that precious child, when the plan or the client is going south. Any question that serves all three purposes is a great question. And it's the right question for you and for the person you serve, whether client, colleague, life partner, child, friend … or whomever.

Practice

1. Think about a happy memory from your childhood. Relive it
    in your mind. Really get into the scene, and see if you can re-
    experience it. Pay attention to how you feel as you recall it.
    Savor the memory—its images, sounds, bodily sensations, feel-
    ings, and interactions with your environment.

    Answer these four questions:

    - What aspects of this childhood memory call out to you?

    - What would be its present-day, adult equivalent for you?

    - How can you give yourself this updated experience?

    - What would that do for you?

        This week, give yourself the gift of recalling this memory for
        a moment, from time to time. A moment of savoring can
        serve as a wonderful oasis for you.

2. Experiment with asking a new client the following question:
    "Would you tell me about a happy memory from your child-
    hood?" See what happens.

3. Experiment with asking the question to family members or
    friends. See what you learn, and see what they learn.

Chapter 10:
Envisioning Your Life Fully Lived

*H*ow do you want to be remembered?

What would you like your legacy to be?

What would you like people to say about you at your funeral service?

Imagine it's ten years in the future, and you're living a full, vibrant, happy life. What is your life like at that time?

These are four wonderful questions for stimulating our thinking about how we want to lead our lives. On a personal level, it's important for all of us to look beyond the details, beyond the joys and sorrows of our present lives, and dare to envision the lives we wish to craft for ourselves. Look at it this way: there are craft shops, there are specialty stores, there are things called artisan breads (whatever those are). Why shouldn't we each craft a wonderful life for ourself? For those of us who work in helping professions such as counseling, coaching, financial planning, education, and the law, we owe it to our clients to engage them in such conversations and guide them in creating clear, vivid, positive statements of what their highest and best lives might look like.

Of course, we can't count on these vision statements, and the resulting plans, to materialize exactly as we specify them. You may have heard expressions such as "Life is what happens when we're busy making plans" and "If you want to make God laugh, tell Him your plans." Nonetheless, we can create an intentional picture of our lives as we aspire for them to become. We can also base that picture on a clear view of our abilities and our potential, a deep honoring of our aspirations, and a bold and daring view of our future. As Helen Keller said, "Life is either a daring adventure, or nothing."

Too many of us have become aspiration-deprived. We have been taught to aim too low, to accept as our mantra "Who do we think we are, anyway?" Marianne Williamson answers that question beautifully in *A Return to Love*:

> Our deepest fear is that we are powerful beyond measure ... We ask ourselves, who am I to be brilliant, gorgeous, talented, fabulous? Actually, who are you NOT to be? ... Your playing small does not serve the world. There is nothing enlightening about shrinking so that other people won't feel unsure around you ... As we let our own Light shine, we unconsciously give other people permission to do the same.

I believe that those of us in helping professions are in a wonderful position to help our aspiration-deprived clients reclaim their right to dream, and to exercise the pursuit of happiness. And we don't have to be professional helpers to do this. In our committed relationships—marriages, life partnerships, and so forth—one of the wonderful ways we can support each other is by holding the flame and keeping the faith as our partners pursue their dreams.

Here are three ways to embrace that right to dream and engage in hot pursuit of happiness.

- In your personal life, imagine, or re-imagine, your future as you wish it to be. Follow up by specifying some goals and actions to get you moving in the direction of your dreams. Be bold and daring in your imagining, and be specific in your goals and actions in pursuit of them.

- In your work with clients, answer these three questions for yourself: Does this person have a vivid, compelling, positive view of where he is headed, and what it will look like when he gets there? Do I know what that picture looks like? Am I basing my service to him on that vision?

- And the same applies to your committed relationships. It's like those public service announcements that say, "It's ten o'clock. Do you know where your children are?" Here, the question, as applied to your intimates, becomes: "Do you know what your partner's dream is?"

If the answer to all or most of these questions is "No," can you work with this person to create a picture of his life fully lived? How would such an image enrich what you two are there to do? How would you get started in that visioning process?

To answer that last question, you can initiate the conversation by using any of the four questions posed at the beginning of this chapter. Or you can search your memory bank for the best questions about a fulfilling life that someone has ever posed to you—or the best ones that you have ever posed to someone else. Alternatively, use your imagination. Grow your own great questions. And have fun with them. The more imagination and creativity you can bring to developing them, the more vibrant and compelling the resulting vision will be.

Practice

1. Imagine that Marianne Williamson had you in mind when she wrote the quoted passage. Ask yourself, "What is she trying to tell me that I need to know?" Think about it. Journal about it. She may be on to something that you need to know.

2. Answer one of the following four questions that most appeals to you.

   • How do you want to be remembered?

   • What would you like your legacy to be?

   • What would you like people to say about you at your funeral service?

   • Imagine it is ten years in the future and you are living a full, vibrant, happy life. What is your life like, at that time?

   Write down your answer or, if you are so inclined, make an artistic representation: a drawing, collage, or sculpture. See what you learn from this activity.

   Then put aside your answer or artistic response for one week. At the end of that time, answer one of the three remaining questions. Compare your responses to the two questions. See what insights this comparison provides.

Chapter 11:
Blessings and the Appreciative Life

*B*lessings play a critical role in our lives. Maybe I should say they play a *blessed* role in our lives. They're an important part of virtually all religious and spiritual traditions, transmitting sacred energies from one party to another. This type of blessing is way of reminding each other and ourselves of our godly natures. One of the meanings of the Hindu greeting *Namaste* is "I bow to the Divine in you.' And heaven knows, these days we need as many reminders of our divine natures as we can summon up.

Besides the spiritual aspects, there are practical reasons for viewing our lives as being filled with blessings. It may seem strange to offer a business case for blessing, but there's sound scientific evidence that feeling blessed leads to an enhanced sense of gratitude and abundance, with beneficial impact on our physical and mental health. For example, studies show that keeping a "gratitude journal" leads to decreased physical symptoms, greater optimism about one's life, and greater energy and enthusiasm.

Since reading about this research, I've incorporated the following practice into my nighttime ritual: after I kiss my wife good night and turn out the lamp on my nightstand, I close my eyes and mentally review three things that went particularly well that day. It's a lovely and appreciative way to close the book on the day. Sometimes I fall asleep before I get in my three gratitudes. When I awaken, there are one or two blessings that demand airtime. In those instances, completing the recitation of the three gratitudes becomes a good way to begin the day.

Real-time gratitude is even more powerful. Tuning in to the drive-by blessings conferred by acts in our daily lives provides an intravenous drip of mental health. This includes blessings given to us, blessings we confer on others, and blessings we observe. Let's look at each kind.

Blessings Given to Us: These are small acts of kindness that come our way. Someone holding a door, someone allowing us the last dessert, someone e-mailing us a piece of news we might need to know … Each of these reminds us that we matter to someone else. These things are real blessings, but they work only if we tune into them. As the sign in the bingo hall reads, "You must be present to win." That applies to blessings as well as other jackpots.

In some Buddhist traditions, the first of the five contemplations recited at the beginning of a meal says, "This food is the gift of the whole universe: the earth, the sky, and much hard work." I love to repeat all five contemplations silently. The first one invites me to pause and reflect on the seed that became the food, the farmer who nurtured it, the migrant worker who picked it, the trucker who transported it, the line worker who assembled the truck, and so on—a wonderful reminder of our dependence on each other. I find that reciting it somehow sweetens my food.

I sometimes forget to recite these beautiful contemplations: a missed opportunity to experience, savor, and honor our mutual dependence on each other and on everything on the planet. As Blanche DuBois says in Tennessee Williams's *A Streetcar Named Desire*, "Whoever you are, I have always depended on the kindness of strangers." So many strangers support us and are vital for our well-being. They are mostly unnamed and unknown to me, but I thank them all and bless them all in this appreciative moment.

If we look with an appreciative intent and an appreciative eye, we will detect the cornucopia of blessings available to us, as well as the plagues of locusts. We always have the choice, however, as to where we shine our lamp. An axiom of the appreciative life is this: whatever we focus on will grow! So, if we feel blessings-deprived, we might start by paying more attention to the ones that come our way.

Being the Giver of the Blessing: There are benefits to being the one who blesses others, through our kindness, our generosity, our expression of our concern. Performing such acts increases our self-esteem and strengthens our perception of our own good nature. I've adopted a practice I learned from Jack Kornfield, a Buddhist teacher and psychologist. He says that once he has the slightest inkling to give something to someone else (no matter how valuable the object or how large the amount of money in question), he follows through on it, ignoring the internal voices second-guessing his generosity.

I resolved to adopt it. I can't say that I do it 100 percent of the time, but I'm up to around 80 or 85 percent, and I have to justify to myself when I hold back on those other occasions. When I give in this manner, I become part of the natural order of things. And I typically accept my holding back when I hear myself say, "Nope, not this time." If I accept my resistance in this way, I usually find its grip loosening, and I wind up giving in accordance with my initial impulse. Boy, do I feel good when that happens! It's like giving myself a blessing, just by the greater ease I feel once I relax into my holding back … as paradoxical as that sounds.

I have another practice, borne of an experience I had as a boy. Whenever I spot money on a floor or sidewalk, I leave it for the next person. Sometimes I even pick it up and then put it down again, to have the experience of imagining the surprised delight on the face of the person who eventually spots it. (I never stick around to witness the discovery, but I always savor the mental image of someone's future delight.) Here's why: One day when I was six years old, I found an extremely shiny silver dollar on the ground near my home, and I immediately saw a blinding jolt of bright light (no doubt the sunlight shining off the coin). I felt a surge of joy and well-being as I scooped up the treasure. Recalling that experience a couple of years ago, I resolved to be the gift-giver at such times. It does my heart good to know I might be passing along a blessing as powerful as the one I received more than a half century ago. The prospect of an unknown stranger's delight is more savory for me than having that extra quarter or five-dollar bill in my pocket.

Truth-in-disclosure time: I haven't been called upon to apply this practice to anything larger than a ten-dollar bill. When it comes to scooping up the money and keeping it, I just may have not discovered my trigger point.

Blessings Observed: Witnessing the door held open for someone else, the dessert offered, and myriad other selfless actions is a great antidote to the cynicism we can so easily fall into. The potency of bearing witness increases if we train ourselves to be on the lookout for such acts: to be what John Howell (*Happiness Is an Inside Job*) calls a good-finder. When I have instructed myself to spend some time being a good-finder—to detect every act of kindness, generosity, good will, or whatever else, in a public place, or even better, performed by my wife and stepson—I find my heart opening and my judgments subsiding.

Living in Wisconsin provides me many opportunities to observe such blessings. Say what you will about Cheeseheads, about the faded glory of the Green Bay Packers, and about our demanding Upper Midwest climate. I've lived and worked in many places and have yet to find as much natural, good-hearted generosity in day-to-day transactions as I have here in my current home state. Must be something in the cheese.

Practice

1. Make this a week of blessings observed. Select one or both of the following practices, and practice for the next seven days:

    *   Keep a nightly gratitude journal. Each evening before bedtime, write down three or more things that happened, or that you have done, for which you feel especially grateful.

    *   Keep a morning gratitude journal instead of, or in addition to, the nightly gratitude journal. When you awaken, write down at least three things in your life for which you feel especially grateful. As you write down each one, summon a vivid mental and emotional image of what you are grateful for.

2. Make the following seven days a week of blessings given. Pay attention to the ways in which you give blessings to others this week. (You might keep a written record, if you are of a mind to.)

    *   Whom do you bless?

    *   For what kinds of actions do you impart blessings?

    *   How do you give blessings? (A simple thank you? Praise? A stated wish for a good day, or for success with an endeavor? A kind act performed for the person?)

    *   How do people respond to your blessings?

    For the first three days, see how many blessings you catch

yourself giving. Don't go out of your way to give blessings. Just note your natural style and frequency of blessing.

Then, for the following four days, apply what you have learned in the first three days, looking for every opportunity to pass out blessings. (Don't despair if you see one and don't capitalize on it. The next one is just moments away, so be alert to it.) See what you learn.

Note: For any of the above practices that you test-drive for a week, if you find yourself benefiting from it, consider extending it for one more week. Proceed on a week-by-week basis, and before you know it, it will become a habit. That's how it works.

3. When someone asks you, "Got a minute?" say "Sure!" Then give the person as much time as he needs, and give whatever is needed. Keep your hand from reaching for the doorknob, and keep your eyes from glancing at your watch. See how giving the person that "minute" enriches him, and enriches you.

Chapter 12:
Appreciative Momentitos

*T*he summer doldrums have struck, and I'm finding it hard to muster writing energy today. However, I've been musing about a lot of things lately, and so I thought, instead of a whole Appreciative Moment, why not empty out the kit bag and write some Appreciative Momentitos?

This follows an honorable tradition. Jimmy Cannon, the great *New York Post* sportswriter of the 1950s and 1960s, titled a weekly column "Nobody Asked Me, But ..." I always looked forward to it with great anticipation. Each weekday evening, my father would bring home the *Post* after work. I'd grab it from his hands and open it to the sports section to see if Jimmy Cannon's banner read "Nobody Asked Me, But ..." Whenever it did, I felt a surge of energy course through me, and I knew I was in for an enjoyable ride. And about ten years ago, Jack Handee wrote a book titled *Thoughtitos: When You Don't Have Time for a Complete Thought*. I never read the book, but I loved the title, and it's stayed with me.

And so, today I don't seem to have the requisite energy and focus to produce a full Appreciative Moment. Perhaps your brain is also in the doldrums, and you might enjoy snacking on some bite-size *momentitos*:

An appreciative experiment: Jackie Kelm wrote a terrific book titled *Appreciative Living: The Principles of Appreciative Inquiry in*

Personal Life. Last year, she did a study of joy and happiness and what promotes these states, and I was one of thirty-four participants. Among the exercises were two that we were asked to do on a daily basis, first thing in the morning. One is gratitude journaling. When I got up, the first thing I did was to write down three things for which I was grateful that day. That was fun, and sometimes a revelation. I tried do it at night as well because I found that I needed that booster shot.

The second exercise, also to be done upon arising, was to create an intention for the day. Specifically, I was instructed to answer the question, "What is one thing, large or small, that I could do today to increase my joy?" I found the latter exercise to be quite powerful. It organized my day for me and gave it a focus and a purpose. It served as a beacon, keeping me on track or getting me back on track at those times when I veered off. (You probably recognize my dysfunctional habits: excessive e-mailing and doing errands that need to be done sometime, so why not do them now instead of attempting the hard work of actually thinking?) Since that time, whenever I'm aware that I'm off task, I simply ask myself, "Now, what was it that I was dedicating the day to?" and instantly I'm back on track. I have continued to do both of these practices since being one of Jackie's research subjects, and I recommend both of these practices to you, preferably to be done in tandem. The gratitude journaling grounds me in joy, contentment, and appreciation, and the beaconing exercise points me in a direction for the day, with clarity and focus. Thanks, Jackie, for your great book, this absorbing study, and your gracious foreword to my book. I am very grateful. Not to mention appreciative.

What's Right with Me? I found this fascinating book at Waldenbooks in Chicago recently, and of course, I just had to buy it. Its entire title is *What's Right with Me? Positive Ways to Celebrate*

Your Strengths, Build Self-Esteem & Reach Your Potential. It's written by a mother-daughter team, Carlene and Carolyn Deroo, and it's quite delicious. The book offers numerous useful questions and exercises that readers can guide themselves through, providing meaningful opportunities to boost their self-esteem. Unlike many other self-help books, which guide their readers into a dark-side dive, this one is uplifting and joyful. Also, the authors sprinkle an array of fabulous quotations from other writers throughout the book. Let me share three of them with you, along with my own associations to them.

Neal Maxwell said, "We can make quiet but honest inventories of our strengths, since, in this connection, most of us are dishonest bookkeepers and need confirming outside auditors." This quotation anticipates the work of Martin Seligman, Donald Clifton, and other positive psychologists who have created "strengths inventories" and conducted important research on strengths, how they cluster together, and what helps us to strengthen them. So much of Appreciative Inquiry focuses on helping us to identify and celebrate our strengths. I think it's possible to be honest and unapologetic internal auditors of our strengths, and I'm not so sure we need to be quiet about them. The noise from the less-generous voices of our inner choirs (and the less-generous segments of our outer world) often requires us to turn up our self-appreciative volume.

Edward Shapiro and Wesley Carr said, "The most important skill is the capacity to learn from individual experiences, our own and others." Absolutely right. No one would survive infancy or childhood without vicarious learning. In one way or another, we're all imprinted ducks … except that, unlike the mallards, we also have minds of our own. Imitation isn't everything. You could say it's not all it's quacked up to be. (Sorry.) Appreciative Inquiry invites us to learn from our stories of individual and collective high point moment experiences, rather than blindly following the lead of others who are held up as the gold standard. It all comes down to balance and judgment.

Jean Shinoda Bolen said, "The choices we make determine who we become, offering us the possibility of leading an authentic life." Yes indeed. I recall that whenever I was confronting a difficult choice, my great mentor, Ruth, would always say, "Remember, Ed, I'm an existentialist. I believe that you are what you do." I agreed with her, though I wasn't always grateful for the reminder. When she would say that (and she always said that at such times), I felt as if I had to make the moral choice, which was often the more difficult path. It took me years to realize that there's an unexplored upside to healthy choosing: our ability to become more *choiceful* brings with it the promise of personal healing, growth, and transformation. I don't think that Ruth would have quarreled with the notion that I am my choices. Choicefulness begins with being awake and aware in the present moment, which is the only moment when we have a choice. (Yes, we can postpone it to a future time, at which point it will be the present moment all over again.) And it's the only time when we can grow. That gives the present moment premier status over all other moments.

Positive Psychology: This is a recent branch of psychology, dedicated to identifying the causes and consequences of positive mental health, healthy families, and positive organizations and communities. How I wish it had been flourishing forty years ago, when I was a psychology graduate student! I'm sure I would have wanted to dedicate my career to helping deepen and expand this important field of inquiry. Whereas most of clinical psychology was consumed in those days with psychopathology, and psychologists studied personality from the starting point of disturbances, positive psychology uses a very different set of lenses. It seeks to focus on the good, the true, and the beautiful. Imagine a book on the psychology of happiness, one on the psychology of savoring, and one on appreciative intelligence. They're all available. Or a whole research program dedicated to investigating the role of positive emotions, and learning how to generate more of them more of the time. It's out there as well. I've been doing a lot of catch-up reading lately in this literature. Plowing through research summaries in this field, as in all of science, typically bores me (research summaries are always as dry as the Gobi Desert), but their findings are terrifically important and need to be broadcast widely. Positive psychology is one of my gratitudes.

Chapter Title of the Year Award: My friend Jim Armstrong wrote a fine book titled *Beyond the Mission Statement.* Jim believes passionately in helping businesses identify their passionate reasons for doing what they do; he helps them go beyond the mission statement (beyond what they do) to identify the cause that they are addressing by their very existence: the *why* of the firm. His book is well worth looking at. (You can find it at www.goodforbusiness.com, which is the Web site of Jim's firm, and at www.paramountbooks.com.) Jim guides readers through ten questions to help them get to their cause, their *why*. I love the title of chapter 9, which is devoted to those questions that get at the cause. He titled it "How to Why." That title is so Jim. While I'm at it, I owe a special debt to Jim and Kathy. They have encouraged the rock band in which my stepson is the lead singer and Michael Armstrong is the drummer, to rehearse in *their* basement. This is worth, in the words of the Old Testament, a price above rubies. Talk about gratitude! Thank you, thank you, thank you!

Practice

1. "We can make quiet but honest inventories of our strengths …" Take the online VIA (Values in Action) Inventory of Strengths developed by Martin Seligman, PhD, and Chris Peterson, PhD. Go to www.viasurvey.org and follow the instructions. The inventory is a self-report questionnaire covering twenty-four character strengths. Allow thirty minutes to complete it, plus time to review the resulting online report, which shows your five highest strengths, describes each one, and compares your scores to the thousands of others who have taken the inventory. When you have reviewed the profile, answer these questions:

   • What aspects of the profile and report confirm what you already knew or believed about your strengths?

   • What surprises were there for you, in terms of your five top VIA profile strengths?

   • What surprises were there, in terms of areas you consider strengths, but that didn't show up in your top five?

   • How does the work you do (or plan to do) align with your top strengths, as identified in your VIA Inventory of Strengths profile?

   • What can you do to bring your work and your strengths into greater alignment?

2. "The choices we make determine who we become, offering us the possibility of leading an authentic life." Think about an important situation in your life in which you were confronted with a difficult choice, and in which you chose well. Write about the situation, including the dilemmas you faced, the alternatives you considered, people who were helpful to you in

addressing your dilemmas, and the choice you made. Keeping in mind the proposition that you are what you do:

- What did the choice you made say about you?
- What did you have to let go of in that situation, in order to make the choice you made?
- In what way did your choice offer you the possibility of leading an authentic life?
- In what ways did making that successful choice help you subsequently to be more choiceful?

Repeat this exercise for two other situations in which you chose well. When you are finished, see if any patterns or themes emerge across the three situations and your choices in them.

Chapter 13:
The Best Kind of Whiplash

*T*his week, I've been totally focused on churning out consulting reports, workshop proposals, learning agreements, and other relatively dense so-called deliverables. All the while, I've had a small, persistent voice continually reminding me that I have a chapter to write. As I sat down to review my lengthy list of possible topics I realized, based on the velocity with which my head was spinning, that I was on serious overload.

Then, as fate would have it, I happened upon a handwritten page with a heading that read, "Ideas that changed my life." Below it, I had written eight or nine phrases depicting ideas, each of which, when I first encountered it, produced what I now think of as appreciative whiplash. On each occasion, my mind did such a double take that I'm surprised I didn't wind up having to wear a neck brace for a month.

Believe it or not, this type of whiplash is actually a wonderful, welcome sensation for me. Some of the greatest learning experiences in my life have taken place when I've been stopped in my tracks by an idea, a revelation, or some other kind of utterance that shakes up my assumptions or, conversely, that allows everything to glide nicely into place. What a wonderful moment that always is for me! I trust I'm not unique in that way. Maybe you've had experiences of this type. I'd like to share three of the ideas that changed my life. They're not likely to change yours, but reading about them might stimulate your thinking about ideas that have stopped you cold and given you appreciative whiplash. If that should happen, I hope you'll savor the recollection.

It's Not What the Behavior is. It's What the Behavior Gets. I can't recall the name of the psychologist who spoke those words at the 1970 Southern California Behavior Modification Conference. I was an academic clinical psychologist at the time, and I was heavily into both behavioral therapies and humanistic psychotherapies. When I heard the presenter declare, "It's not what the behavior is. It's what the behavior gets," my mind did a backflip. "Yes," I said, "that's exactly what reinforcement is all about!" It was such an elegant and economical way to express how easily we can be misled and seduced by the form of what someone is doing, and that we fail to note how the consequences of the act reward the person for performing it.

This can explain quite a lot about attention-getting behaviors like physical complaints (so-called hypochondria), classroom clowning (George Carlin said, "Being class clown means 'Hell, I'm not learning anything; time to disrupt someone else's education!'"), and even some forms of gang violence. Gang members have been known to say, "It's better to be wanted by the police than not to be wanted at all." Let me be clear here: I'm not claiming that "It's not what the behavior is. It's what the behavior gets" explains all of our behaviors and experiences. No one thing does. But it's an eloquent reminder about an important aspect of life, and it's clearly worth putting on a refrigerator magnet, if you are inclined to do such a thing.

We are Already Very Rich. I was attending a dharma talk at Insight Meditation Society (IMS) in Barre, Massachusetts, a few years ago, as part of a weeklong retreat. The dharma teacher, a lovely woman named Myoshin Kelly, was talking to the seventy-five of us about abundance, in the spiritual and emotional senses of the term.

A little context would be helpful here. Dharma teachers like Myoshin, who follow the Buddhist tradition, do not draw salaries. They survive, as did the Buddha and his followers, on *dana* (pronounced dah-na) which, in the Pali language, means generosity. Listeners who feel enriched by the teachings donate money or goods to the dharma teacher so she can support herself and perpetuate the teaching tradition. *Dana* strikes me as being a wonderful tradition.

Myoshin and her husband, Richard, who was IMS's executive director at the time, were probably just getting by, financially speaking. She told us the story of the time when Richard and she were reflecting, with some anxiety, on their financial situation, and noting ruefully that they would never accumulate financial wealth. As they stood looking out over the beautiful IMS grounds in the fullness of the New England autumn, and perhaps taking a mental inventory of all they did have, Richard turned to her and said simply, "We are already very rich." And Myoshin said to us, equally simply, "And he was right." I agree.

All He Has to Do is Be Himself. One evening, some years ago, when Jody and I were still engaged, she was talking with her son, Aman (now seventeen years old, but at that time, just shy of his eleventh birthday). She mentioned to him, as she told me a day or two later, that I'd been having some concerns about whether I could be a good stepfather, given that I'd never had children and didn't know anything about being in a parenting role. Without skipping a beat, Aman looked at her and said, "All he has to do is be himself."

How did he get to be so smart, so early? You're not supposed to say things like that until you're thirty-eight. (I looked it up.)

As you might imagine, I was stopped in my tracks when Jody related the story. I just shook my head in wonder at the simplicity and profundity of his words. I must confess that being myself with my stepson hasn't always meant manifesting the better angels of my nature. However, I've worked hard to identify, appreciate, and build on those better angels, and I am (and we are) reaping dividends. Aman's a wonderful guy, we're getting along better all the time, and I can't tell you how often his sage advice—as relayed by Jody that day long ago—has stood me in good stead in various walks of my life, not only in stepparenting him. When I'm stumped about what to do in a situation where all my experience, devices, and mantras seem to be failing me, I sometimes recall Aman's words of wisdom, and I relax into whatever being myself means in that moment. Those words of wisdom have never let me down. So I want to offer them to you, for whatever riches they may confer. Here they are: all you have to do is be yourself.

Practice

1. Recall phrases, aphorisms, and words of wisdom that produce a case of appreciative whiplash in you. For each, think about its meaning for you, and how it has influenced your life. Have you paid it forward? That is, have you passed along those pearls to others, by word or deed? If not, how could you do so?

2. "It's not what the behavior is, it's what the behavior gets." Think of a behavior that someone in your family or your work environment does that is vexing, puzzling, or troubling for you. Answer these three questions:

- What do you and others do immediately after the person performs that behavior?

- What would be the most effective alternative way of responding?

- What do you imagine might happen if you responded that way?

  Consider adopting that alternative response the next few times the behavior recurs. See what happens.

3. "We are already rich." Scan through your life as it is today. Identify all the ways in which you are already rich. Make a list of these sources of abundance.

  - As you go through your week, be alert to the various ways in which you are already rich.

  - Review your own list each morning or evening.

  - Ask members of your family to make their own abundance lists, and share them together.

4. "All he has to do is be himself." Reflect on how this statement applies to you. Then answer these two questions:

  - What happens inside you and around you when you are being yourself?

  - How can you be yourself more of the time?

  Let these questions rattle around within you this week. Note the answers that arise. Heed their call. See what happens.

Chapter 14:
The Art of Savoring

I've been musing lately about *savoring*. It's such a delicious topic that I've been finding it, well, savory. I want to share some thoughts about it, explore why we should bother to savor, and encourage you to cultivate this appreciative art. In the next two chapters, I'll have more to say about this mouth-watering topic.

Savoring is defined as the awareness of pleasure, and the devoting of deliberate attention to that experience. You can savor positive experiences before they happen (anticipating), while they're happening (real-time savoring), and after they happen (reminiscing). Fred Bryant and Joseph Veroff, psychologists at Loyola University of Chicago, describe four types of savoring:

- **Basking:** receiving praise and congratulations from others

- **Thanksgiving:** expressing gratitude for blessings

- **Marveling:** losing the self in the wonder of the moment

- **Luxuriating:** indulging the senses

My experience in writing the columns upon which this book is based has taught me a lot about these four flavors of savoring.

- Each week, I've received unsolicited words of praise and thanks from quite a few readers, for benefits and blessings that they found in these writings. I've loved receiving and reading those words of thanks. In fact, I've basked in them. Call me self-centered if you like. But call me often.

- I've always felt enriched and honored by readers' responses. They've always been a blessing for me, and I have gathered them in with grateful thanksgiving. I try to convey my thanks to all who respond. Readers' responses have emboldened me to continue, expand, and deepen the whole venture, and to write this book. A big *thank you*!

- Sometimes the responses come in so fast, and have been so moving, that I simply stop to marvel at what I seem to have set in motion. It's bigger than I am, and I see myself as a vehicle for transmitting these words and thoughts, from wherever they emanate. As Jack Kornfield, the Buddhist teacher and psychologist, says about the mysterious source of his own writings and those of other spiritual teachers, "Clearly, we're all just taking dictation." And that zany madman Mel Brooks once did a routine in which he portrayed a wildly popular singer named Fabiola. Asked by Carl Reiner to explain the source of his popularity, Fabiola said, "We are all singing. I have the mouth." I often feel that way about the columns, and I love the call-and-response quality to the ongoing conversations with readers.

- The more eloquent responses, such as the one about being invited up to the farm, which appears in chapter 18, were so richly detailed that I was transported into luxuriating, as though I were actually there with the e-mail writer. As you may find when you read his letter about wanting to be invited up to the farm, luxuriating is a glorious experience.

A sad and perplexing note: I have noticed that some people are basking-impaired. In my coaching, consulting, presentations, and workshops, I sometimes encounter folks who are unable to acknowledge positive feedback without visibly writhing, or who can't brag about themselves and their accomplishments. (The great actor Jimmy Stewart was the epitome of the strong, silent, socially awkward man who would dig a hole in the dirt with the toe of his cowboy boot and say, "Shucks, ma'am, 'tweren't nuthin'.") Invariably, I have found these people to be prodigiously talented, highly accomplished, and very effective in their work lives. Their basking impairment goes well beyond simply being well-mannered. I don't think I could pay them enough to get them to be the center of attention and appreciation. They'd sooner curl up and die. Sad, isn't it? These wonderful people contribute so much to the rest of us, yet they remain impoverished in the vital area of self-appreciation.

Some regard savoring as a self-indulgent practice, reserved for baby boomers as we enter our otherwise-declining years. Perhaps you worry that there's something vaguely narcissistic about how much you enjoy savoring food, praise, sex, or the universe as a whole. If so, perhaps you can take comfort in the words of a monk who once told me, "Everything in moderation, Ed ... including moderation."

If you need a business case for savoring, in order to justify it for yourself or others, consider this: savoring is a positive emotional experience, and positive emotions have been scientifically shown to produce many important outcomes for persons and organizations. For example, they

- enhance individual, interpersonal, and group mood, leading to more productive interactions and outcomes;

- deepen interpersonal and group relationships;

- expand the number of ideas and actions for consideration;

- increase creativity and problem solving;

- strengthen resilience (the ability to absorb multiple changes, and to bounce back and learn from adversity).

In short, savoring isn't simply narcissistic, and it isn't just something you do before you get to the real agenda. Cultivating savoring is a highly effective business (and personal) strategy for getting so-called real work done. That is reason enough to be intentional about the following: (a) beginning meetings with an appreciative question; (b) inquiring into each others' stories of highest and best moments; (c) extending gratitude to others (and to ourselves); and (d) performing other appreciative practices that promote savoring. To put it in boldly capitalist terms, savoring is a highly leveraged investment! My advice to you is this: savor often and with zest, and reap a high ROS (return on savoring). Remember, everything in moderation ... including moderation.

Here are several questions to ponder and to help you along the path of savoring: Are you investing enough time in slowing down and smelling the roses, the coffee, the many and varied fragrances of life? When are you best at basking, thanksgiving, marveling, luxuriating? When do these seem to be unaffordable frivolities? Note that these latter times are your greatest opportunities to turn the corner on your habits of savoring. Make the most of these opportunities. Practice random acts of intentional savoring and see what happens.

Practice

This week, take time to slow down and savor the tastes, smells, textures, sounds, and feelings of your life.

- Spend the first two days getting a baseline. Be like a camera, taking in the landscape of savoring. Notice when you are taking time to bask, to give thanks, to marvel in the wonder of the moment, and to luxuriate indulgently in a sense pleasure. Simply pay attention to the variety of ways in which you savor your life. Also pay attention to when you pass up savoring opportunities coming your way. These two days, just notice. Don't strive to change a thing.

- For the rest of the week, each time you become aware of an opportunity, practice a moment of savoring. As often as feasible, allow yourself that moment of basking, thanksgiving, marveling, or luxuriating. Notice how these various savory moments feel, and how they influence your day.

  - **Mindfulness Tip 1:** Be gentle and kind with yourself when you let savoring opportunities pass you by. You'll learn something as valuable from these missed occasions as from the savory occasions you allow yourself. Simply ask yourself, "What can I do to take advantage of these opportunities? How can I savor the very next opportunity that comes my way?"

  - **Mindfulness Tip 2:** Practice savoring in the same manner that native-born Chicagoans used to instruct me on how to vote when I lived there—early and often.

Chapter 15:
My Father's Photographs

There's some fascinating and useful research emerging in the field of positive psychology, on how to nurture our habits of savoring. I would love to tell you about these findings, but I have a problem. Research findings are as dry and boring to read as their implications are important and exciting to know about. So instead of reporting on them here, I thought I'd tell you a story of an event that I savored at the time, that I savor as I recollect it, and that I'll savor as I write it here. In the next chapter, I'll show how the research findings of Fred Bryant and Joe Veroff of Loyola University of Chicago apply to the story I'm about to relate. My hope is that reading the story of the last time I saw my father will bring their five recommended practices to life, to help guide you in your own savoring practice.

It was early July 1983, and I was visiting my father in a hospital in Fort Lauderdale, where he was not expected to last the weekend. He was in the final throes of lymphoma, was heavily medicated, and was not very lucid. However, he seemed to rally when he saw me appear at the door of his room, along with my favorite aunt, his sister Sally, who lived close by. Aunt Sally and I visited him often those next two days. On Sunday morning, we found a shoebox filled with my father's old photos (some dating back fifty years or more) in his condo, and we lovingly arranged them in two albums as a present. Sally and I deeply savored both the experience of organizing them and the gleeful anticipation of giving them to him later that afternoon.

A little background would be helpful here. My dad was a wonderful amateur photographer, but he resembled the TV detective Adrian Monk when it came to posing us for family pictures. The phrase *glacial pace* comes to mind. It took him an eternity to arrange the lighting, the composition, and the exposure settings, to his exacting requirements. We must have resembled a family tableau in Madame Tussaud's Wax Museum by the time we finally heard the long-awaited click of his box camera. Then, like Sisyphus rolling the boulder up the hill, the process began all over again. I don't savor reminiscing about or recounting those ordeals. The opposite of savoring is *enduring*. We endured, but we didn't endure gracefully. Nonetheless, this background will help you to more fully understand the remarkable story that was about to unfold among the three of us that Sunday afternoon in Dad's hospital room.

Sally and I took the photo albums to the hospital for my final visit before leaving for the airport, and we showed them to my father. Or, I should say, he showed them to us. He brightened considerably when he opened an album to the first page and encountered four ancient photos. This process of brightening continued to unfold as he treated us to an impromptu narrative: for each photograph, he told us exactly when he took it, named the people who were in it, described how he posed them, and offered any other details that we cared to hear. And of course, we cared to hear all the details, every last one. We savored every drop of his narrative, and we doubly savored his restored vitality and animation as he rallied for this breathtaking farewell performance.

In the middle of the show, I spontaneously stopped him and said, with genuine admiration, "Dad, these are great photographs!" He looked puzzled, even stunned, for a long moment. Finally, he said, with a perplexed look that I'll never forget, "But you all were always so mad at me." I pondered his assertion for a moment and replied, "Oh, we still are ... but these are great photographs!" Well, you should have heard the three of us laughing uproariously. It was a sweet moment for all of us, and one that I savor as I recount it now. When our laughter finally subsided, he resumed the show. And here's the amazing finale: by the end of the afternoon visit, he was so revitalized that after I hugged and kissed him good-bye, and was almost out the door, I heard him exclaim, "Wait!"

Startled, I turned around and looked at him.

"It's your birthday!" he said.

Surprised that he had remembered, I replied, simply, "Yes."

"Happy birthday, son," he said.

I smiled, said, "Thanks, Dad," and left.

What a birthday gift! It was the best gift and, sadly, the last one, he ever gave me.

Those were the last words we ever exchanged in person. Dad died several months later. I can't overstate the blessings that he bestowed on me, and on Sally, in that hospital room that Sunday: the gift of his narration, the gift of his rallying, the gift of his remembering my birthday, and the gift of his birthday wish for me. Sally and I savored the recounting of it all as she drove me to the airport. And as I replay the story in my mind, and as I find the words to relate it here, I find myself savoring it all over again and luxuriating in the opportunity to share it with you. Despite the virtual nature of communicating with unseen readers in books or in cyberspace, it's as though we are arrayed around a campfire, and I'm spinning a tale to absorb and mesmerize you. So thank you for being the readers and listeners. As poet Muriel Rukeyser (*The Speed of Darkness*) writes, "The universe is made of stories, not atoms."

Practice

1. Take a five-minute trip back in time and recall a precious memory: an occasion rich with meaning, importance, and deep feelings. Vividly recollect the time and the setting. In your mind's eye, place yourself in the situation. Hear the sounds, smell the smells, see the sights, taste the tastes, etc. Allow yourself to fully savor them. When you are done, notice how the story, and your savoring of it, has enriched you.

    Whenever you need a bit of self-nourishment, take a trip to that time or to another precious memory. Spend a couple of minutes savoring the experience, and then come back, refreshed and revitalized. Rather than thinking of it as an escape or avoidance, consider that it is an important stillpoint (a term used by Dr. David Kundtz in *Stopping*, to describe a brief respite that he recommends we give ourselves frequently). When you need a stillpoint, take it. And savor it.

2. Share the above trip-back-in-time practice with family members and/or friends. Allow everyone, including yourself, sufficient time to silently recall and savor their own stories. Then take turns sharing the stories. Savor telling your own story and savor hearing others' stories. After each has taken a turn, invite everyone to talk about the experience. Simply ask, "How was that for you?"

Chapter 16:
Improve Your Savoring Quotient

*T*his past weekend, Jody asked me if writing the story that I told in the previous chapter, about my dad, Aunt Sally, and the photographs had brought back the experience vividly. "Yes … and no" was my answer. I explained that I had been so focused on writing the story that my intense concentration lessened my sense of feeling immersed it. However, in the process of writing, I kept being bombarded with images, pictures, and sensations from the events of that day. So, while I can't say I was immersed in the experience, I was peppered by a stream of recollections. That sense of being peppered served as a container that held me lovingly and supportively while I wrote. That same sense of being held has continued, though naturally it has waned as the days have passed.

Our conversation got me thinking about Fred Bryant and Joe Veroff's research on processes that promote savoring. Here are the five techniques that their research has found to increase the pleasure of an event and one's awareness of that pleasure. As you read each, see if it matches up with your own experience, and if it might be something that you would like to do more of to increase your SQ (your savoring quotient).

Sharing the Experience With Others: This may involve commenting on the experience and how enjoyable it is while it's taking place. It also can entail telling the story afterward, and relating how much you enjoyed it. This is the most powerful factor revealed in their research. I think it's what Jody was getting at with her question. Writing about and sharing the experience with an invisible reading community did bring back the experience quite vividly. It was a gift that kept on giving, with ongoing recalls during the ensuing week. Sharing the experience with others stimulates memories, which stimulates the production of brain chemicals similar to those produced during the event itself. It's akin to executing the Refresh command on your computer. Perhaps that's why we say that the memory is so vivid that it feels as though we're back in the experience; to our brains, there is little difference.

Memory Building: This consists of Kodak moments (i.e., photographs, video recordings, and the like), as well as physical mementos of the event, which are reminisced about later. Certainly, the photo albums, one of which I still have, help preserve and refresh the event for me. Also, when my brothers and I went back to Florida for the funeral, and to pack up Dad's belongings, I kept his watch as a keepsake. Funny thing: it wasn't working then, it still doesn't work, and it weighs a ton compared with more modern timepieces. Yet it has a place of honor atop the two-drawer file cabinet in my office, and I look at it at least once or twice a day. It's reassuring and comforting. The face still reads 3:24. Some things, at least, don't change.

Sharpening Perceptions: This process is akin to the meditative process of concentration, in which one focuses on a single aspect of experience to the exclusion of all others. At a concert, for example, you may find yourself immersed in the sound of the strings. Similarly, while eating a wonderful meal, you may tune out the social conversation while tuning into the taste of the food. (You may not be invited back, but you'll have fond and vivid memories of the eats.) I used this process of sharpening my perceptions at one point in the hospital room, by focusing on how gorgeous the photos were. I completely tuned out the conversation for a time because I was so entranced by the beauty of the photographs.

Absorption: This is the process of fully immersing yourself in the sensory experience itself, rather than thinking or talking about it. Absorption is akin to the meditative process of mindfulness, i.e., moment-to-moment awareness of sensations going on around and within you. In the hospital room with my father and aunt, I felt fully engaged, but not fully absorbed. I was too busy thinking about the stories my dad was telling, the people he was describing, and occasionally, how soon I would need to leave for the airport, to be fully absorbed. Absorption is a wonderful practice for enhancing the experience of savoring. Many of us, though, find it difficult to become absorbed because we're more verbally, socially, or cognitively oriented than we are sensually oriented. While each of these three orientations has its own considerable strengths, each one detracts from the ability to lose oneself in the experience. For example, I am so verbally oriented (Jody says that on a one-to-ten scale, I am a fifteen) that I need to exert conscious effort to savor the experience, rather than translate it into words.

Self-congratulation: This final process is one which some of you may find difficult. Self-congratulation is the act of giving yourself positive self-talk when you receive praise or an award, or when a milestone event has occurred and you tell yourself how hard you've worked to bring it about. A certain amount of frank self-congratulation is healthy for individuals, families, and organizations. Without it, we fail to see our true place in the world, and to fully grasp what we have contributed by exercising our gifts. This void can make our life into a dry, lifeless ordeal. Garrison Keillor's depiction of the Minnesota bachelor farmer, on the radio program *A Prairie Home Companion*, is the stereotype of this pattern. Shouldn't we be equally as adept and comfortable about self-congratulation as we are about celebrating other people's contributions and achievements? Correspondingly, shouldn't we be able to bask in others' congratulations and praise, as noted in chapter 14? Making ourselves smaller than our true size doesn't make anyone else bigger, and it certainly diminishes us.

On the other hand, too much self-congratulation verges on self-absorption. I'm reminded of the title of David Brinkley's memoir: *Everyone Is Entitled to My Opinion*. We're all finely tuned to detect when someone has crossed the dividing line into self-absorption, though we may need others' help in knowing when we ourselves have crossed the line. Perhaps that's what marriage and other intimate partnering relationships are for.

I wonder if these five processes for enhancing savoring apply to you. If so, I wonder if they facilitate your ability to appreciate (i.e., to savor) your experiences and your life. Have Bryant and Veroff nailed savoring for you? (Check out practice 1 below to find out.)

What would it take for you to raise your Savoring Quotient, and thereby enhance your quality of life? As noted earlier, the poet Rilke wrote, in *Letters to a Young Poet*, "Live the questions." Of course, positive psychology didn't exist in 1903. If he were writing today, Rilke might well have expressed the thought as "Savor the questions."

Practice

Here are a couple of questions to answer, with the goal of increasing your savoring quotient (SQ).

1. Think about the five savoring practices that Bryant and Veroff have identified:

   - Sharing the experience with others
   - Memory building
   - Sharpening perceptions
   - Absorption
   - Self-congratulation

   Rank these five practices from one to five, according to which one you use most frequently (rate it a one), next most frequently (give it a two), and so forth.

   - Which savoring practice did you rate as a one (most frequently used)? What is its greatest benefit for you?

   - Which one did you rate a five (least frequently used)? What would be some potential benefits of using that least practiced practice more often? What steps can you take to increase your use of it? Here are some helpful hints for traversing this road less traveled:

     - **Helpful Hint 1:** Call to mind some people who are positive role models of using that practice. Visualize them using that approach. See if it resonates with you, and if it's something you can adopt or adapt to your own style.

     - **Helpful Hint 2:** In the coming week, keep alert to occasions where you see someone using that practice. Note how it works out, and ask yourself if it has potential for you.

     - **Helpful Hint 3:** Catch yourself using that practice and when you do, practice Self-congratulation.

2. For each of the five savoring practices, think of a time when you enjoyed using it to savor an experience. Recall the circumstances, whom you were with, how you used that practice, and how it worked for you. For each story, ask the following questions:

    - What would it take to use that practice (e.g., sharing the experience, memory building, etc.) more of the time?
    - What would you gain from doing that?

Chapter 17:
Feedback: The Ultimate Grow Light

*T*he idea for this chapter came to me one wintry Tuesday evening while listening to Jane Hamilton read from her startling novel, *When Madeline Was Young*, at Borders West here in Madison. More precisely, it came to me while Jane was telling all one hundred and fifty of us about the time, many years ago, when she hesitatingly read a draft of her short story to a group of her fellow writing students. (She lives in Rochester, Wisconsin, which makes us neighbors. I figure I'm entitled to refer to her as Jane.)

It turns out her hesitancy was well grounded. The students, probably following their instructor's lead and the group's norm, heaped generous servings of well-meaning criticism (and isn't that an oxymoron!) upon her and the story. No doubt they found every possible weakness in the writing, and I suspect they weren't crazy about her shoes either. Naturally, she was devastated by the feedback. She pointed out to us, with remarkable evenhandedness, that she didn't feel the comments were unjust, simply that they had hurt. They also dealt a crushing blow to any intention she might have entertained about reading any future work before it was ready for prime time. She now reads her novels-in-the-making to her husband, who takes it all in with great patience and caring, though she knows he would rather simply read her written words. How's that for love?

Jane's story about constructive criticism took me back to my own experience in numerous writing workshops with my writing teacher and friend, Hal Zina Bennett, and my experience as a member of a long-running writing group of his students. Without referring to Appreciative Inquiry, positive psychology, or any other theory or approach, Hal taught us, by word and deed, the art of appreciative feedback. We were carefully guided to listen with the heart to each others' writings. When we read what we had written in response to one of Hal's exercises, the only feedback we were allowed to give was appreciative: Where were we moved by the writing? Where did the writing bring up feelings and sensations within us? Where did the writing take us? Where were we inspired?

Hal's theory is that this kind of feedback tells the writer where the juice is in his writing, and his marvelous book, *Write From the Heart*, is aptly named. (Give his Web site, www. halzinabennett.com, a look.) Hal intuitively knows that whatever we focus on will grow, and that if we use appreciative feedback to teach each other where our writing gifts lie, those gifts will be nurtured, and they will grow and thrive. So each time we read aloud, we were lavishly treated to feedback about where the writing took our listeners. The feedback didn't just feel good. It also inspired, motivated, affirmed, and instructed us. Our writing grew as a result, and so did we.

I think Hal's theory is applicable to not only the craft of writing, but virtually everywhere else as well. If you've ever been a parent (or a child, for that matter), you know that every day brings with it dozens of opportunities to respond to what kids do. Or to what spouses or partners do. Or work associates. Or softball teammates. Do we practice listening from the heart? Do we find and make a big deal about the person's gifts, talents, achievements, generosity, resilience, genius, aspirations, and so on? Or do we listen to "helpfully" point out what's wrong, weak, defective, missing—like

Jane's fellow graduate students? If you've ever set foot in a graduate school seminar, you know what I mean. It's usually a hothouse of mutual constructive criticism. *Mutual assured destruction* may be a better term for it.

Conversely, I have the privilege of sitting at the feet of a master of appreciative feedback every single day. Watching my wife relate to her seventeen-year-old son is like watching Eric Clapton or Itzhak Perlman plying his craft. Jody can take virtually any situation that Aman reports, any intention he declares, or anything he does, and meet it with appreciative intent. She will praise his singing and guitar playing, pointing out what she especially loves and asking him to sing or play it again for her. If I happen to wander by, she beckons me to sit a while and listen. I always do; I'm no dummy. If he's distressed about something (and what seventeen-year-old isn't at least occasionally distressed?), she will listen intently, quietly point out his proven strengths that are relevant to mastering the situation, and either offer a suggestion as to how he might apply those gifts or, if she reads in his eyes that he's got it, leave it alone. And in those areas where we would like him to do something that better suits us (does any adolescent meet his parents' standards of neatness?), she manages to frame it as both a request *and* an expectation, attaches a time line, and doesn't make a big deal about it. And most of the time, it gets done.

I've watched this marvelous young man develop and flourish under her grow light. Nobody can seem to get enough of Aman. He's like "The Mighty Quinn" in Bob Dylan's song of the same name. Here's the key lyric: "But When Quinn the Eskimo gets here/Ev'rybody's gonna jump for joy." It's like that with Aman.

Who are your teachers and master practitioners of appreciative feedback? How have you flourished under their grow lights? Who grows under the loving light of your lamp? And what can you do today to shine that light?

Practice

1. Think about the master practitioners of appreciative feedback you have experienced or observed. What did they do that was masterful? What effect did their appreciative feedback have on you or others?

    -   Identify two or three of their masterful ways that you'd like to adopt. Try them out and see what happens. Practice 2 provides a roadmap for detecting opportunities to perform these masterful acts.

2. Today, covertly be a strength-finder. Let everyone you interact with or observe be your instructor about her strengths. With clients, colleagues, family, friends, and others, be on the look-out for what they are doing well, effectively, or correctly. Make a mental inventory of the strengths they are exhibiting.

    -   Each time you catch them in the act, give them appreciative feedback, the way one of your master practitioners would. Observe what happens. And note your level of comfort or discomfort in offering them such feedback. Remember that when it comes to being a good-finder and an appreciative "feedbacker," imitation is the sincerest form of flattery. Don't worry if at first you feel a little wooden doing so. You'll quickly get more graceful at it. That's the way it works.

Chapter 18:
And I Want to Be Invited up to the Farm

I love stories. One of the great pleasures I derive from writing, making presentations, giving workshops, coaching, and finding other ways of bringing appreciation to my work and life, is hearing or reading the stories people tell me. For example, I read an extraordinary story in an e-mail I received shortly after a presentation I did about a year ago. I was moved and awestruck when I first read it. I've read it repeatedly since that time, always with an ever-deepening sense of awe and astonishment. Although my mind has produced many ways to write about it here, I'm going to resist the temptation to say anything at all. I'd be diverting you from your fresh reading and your unadorned responses, and depriving you of access to the one teacher who can show you the story's real lessons: that teacher, of course, is you. So without further ado, here is the anonymous (by the author's own preference) e-mail:

> I combined Appreciative Inquiry with mind mapping with a client who had given me a hard time about putting together a simple budget. I had been prodding him for over a year to get it done. In my desk, I had prepared a $750 check made out to him. I was willing (maybe even anxious) to refund his deposit just to get rid of him and his self-indulgent spendthrift wife. I first greeted him as if he were my best friend; this to adjust my

attitude more than his. I then told him that I felt I was the reason for his procrastination, and that I would like to take some time to try to understand better how I might be able to help him. I asked his permission to try a fun exercise to help both of us discover what his ultimate objectives might be. I asked him to travel into the future. I wrote in the center of a blank sheet of paper, "I am completely successful." I asked him to draw spokes from the center and write at least several, but unlimited, elements of that success; to write what life looks like now that he is completely successful.

In just five minutes, my perception of him changed dramatically. Until this, I had no idea who I was talking to, and at some level, he knew it. I was very impressed by his future world, especially after drilling deeper on each of the issues, like asking, "What is it about owning this farm that brings you such happiness?" He answered, "It's a place where all my friends and family come to be together and have good times." Note the present tense. He was actually there, in his mind's eye! And what was I learning? His deepest held values! His values flooded out as I AI'd him regarding each of his notations. He shared things so intimate that he didn't even want me to share them with his wife. At least not yet. He asked me to repeat the exercise privately with his wife, just as I had done with him. He enthusiastically agreed to finish preparing the budget with his wife within one week.

Two main things happened. He will never go elsewhere for his financial planning. And I will not abandon him again. He and his wife have a beautiful future waiting, and I want to be invited up to the farm.

I suggest that you reread the story, either now or sometime later. See where each reading takes you. That's what I do periodically. Each time I reread it, I stand in awe of his account and of the greatness of spirit it took for this financial planner to show up for his client as he did. And of his deep skills as a storyteller.

Practice

Try the exercise that was described in the quoted passage above:

On a sheet of blank paper, draw a circle in the center, and inside the circle, write the words, "I am completely successful" (or, if you prefer, "completely fulfilled," "completely content," "completely rich," or another adjective). Imagine it is now three years in the future, and you *are* completely successful (or whatever). Draw spokes out from the center, each one depicting one aspect of your life in three years. If there are other spokes that radiate from a spoke, draw them and label them. When you are done, step back from the portrait of your future life. Answer these seven questions:

1. What strikes you about your portrait?

2. What surprises you about it?

3. Is there anything missing from it?

4. In what areas of your richly imagined life are you already underway, if not quite there?

5. What actions can you commit to in order to live this portrait more fully?

6. Who else can help?

7. How will you enlist other people's help?

Chapter 19:
Give Yourself a Good Talking-To

"Yer gonna make me give myself a good talkin' to."

I love that lyric from Bob Dylan's *You're Gonna Make Me Lonesome When You Go*. For a long time, I've been able to find a Dylan line for just about any situation, to capture virtually any feeling, thought, or nuance. (How about this one-line short story: "Johnny's in the basement/Mixing up the medicine/I'm on the pavement/Thinking about the government.") If I can't find a Dylan lyric to fit a situation, it probably means I haven't kept current on his work.

And so when that Dylan lyric played in my mind this morning, this chapter came together in a flash: the Dylan setup line, the notion of giving oneself a verbal upbraiding, the reframe of giving oneself a verbal caress, and the prospect of bringing in good science about positive talk and positive emotion. It's all too delicious to resist. So here goes:

I'm disturbed and saddened at the huge disservice—the carnage, really—that we do by the ways we talk to ourselves. I'm not the first one to say that if a friend talked to us the way we sometimes give ourselves a good talking-to, we wouldn't want to have anything further to do with this so-called friend. We'd fire the person—if we had any self-respect. But we can't simply fire ourselves. As Jon Kabat-Zinn's book title tells it, *Wherever You Go, There You*

Are. There's a lot written in psychology texts, self-help books, and religious and spiritual literature about the thoughts we carry around about each other, and the suffering they bring all of us. It's all true, but for now, my heart aches for the damage we call down upon the one person in the whole world that each of us is in the best position to love, cherish, and help: ourself.

There is a way out of the merciless self-punishment, self-loathing, and hypercriticism that is, for some among us, our inner soundtrack. As with so much else in life, the way out is by going in: by paying mindful attention to the soundtrack and truly waking up, not to the truth of our self-pronouncements, but to their harshness, to how unrelenting and reflexive they are, and to how tyrannical our inner voices can be. So, I suppose the first step is to "give ourselves a good *listening*-to." Can we tune in, with both indignation and tenderness, to our voice of negativity and ask ourselves, "Is this any way to treat someone I care about?" Developing the skill of getting that millisecond of distance in which to ask ourselves that question is a big step toward liberation. And it's a step we must be prepared to take repeatedly. Victor Frankl said it most eloquently in *Man's Search for Meaning*: "Between stimulus and response, there is a space. In that space lies our freedom and power to choose our response. In our response lies our growth and freedom."

A next step is to track the balance of positive and negative talk you visit upon yourself. This step may sound mechanical and preposterous. Nonetheless, please try it today. At various points throughout the day, tune in to your inner radio frequency and listen to what you're broadcasting to yourself about yourself. Let's say, for example, that you can't locate your keys when you're in a rush to leave. Do you berate yourself ("You've done it again!"), put pressure on yourself ("I'll be screwed if I'm late!"), respond calmly

("Hmm. Where did I see my keys last?"), or react in some other manner?

Believe it or not, you'll learn a lot by getting a handle on your balance of positive-to-negative self-broadcasts. There's good behavioral science about the talk ratio in marriage and in organizations, so why shouldn't we apply it to ourselves? The only things we have to gain are self-esteem and peace.

For example, John Gottman's twenty-plus-years research program on marriage has shown that in healthy, thriving unions, the positive-to-negative talk ratio is five (or more) to one. When the ratio is closer to one to one, the couple is on a slippery slope to divorce. Barbara Fredericksen and Marcial Losada recently published some fascinating organizational research on positive and negative emotions in healthy and dysfunctional organizations. They confirmed their proposition that in healthy, profitable companies, that ratio is three to one or more. Again, a one to one ratio characterizes underperforming corporations, much as it characterizes underperforming marriages. (Interestingly, they found that when the organization's ratio of positive-to-negative emotions exceeds eleven to one, it's not healthy. With that preponderance of positives, the company is papering over its differences, much like our national political parties during their quadrennial circus known as the nominating convention.)

What's your inner ratio? Is there a positive balance? Are you overwhelmed with negative entries? I don't have in mind a specific ratio (for example, four to one or six to one) for you to aim for, but whatever your ratio is, strive to make it positive and high. At times, you may need to dig deep to find something positive about yourself. If so, then put on your Nikes and just do it. Become a Scientist of Yourself and check out your ratio. Experiment with artificially increasing the positives. Think of it this way. You learned, early in your life, to overemphasize the negative side. You can relearn and rebalance your portfolio of self-talk. If the prospect of deliberately thinking up self-compliments sounds unduly self-absorbed, answer this question: who is more absorbed than the person in the midst of a self-administered verbal whipping?

Dylan was right, as usual. After I finish writing this chapter, I'm gonna give myself a good talkin' to. I'll use a ratio of at least three to one.

Care to join me?

Practice

1. For the next couple of days, pay attention to how you talk to yourself. Tune in to the Muzak of your mind, as you would tune into a radio broadcast. Don't get wrapped up in whether what you're hearing is true, false, or otherwise. Your job is just to tune in as an anthropologist might. Don't do anything with it just yet.

    *   Notice how you talk to yourself about yourself: what you say to yourself about your qualities, your actions, your place in the world. Get a feel for your ratio of positive-to-negative self-talk.

    *   Notice how you talk to yourself about others. Is there kindness in it? Envy? Anger? Gratitude? Judgment? What other qualities are in there? What's the positive-to-negative ratio in your self-talk about these people?

2. After a couple of days, decide if you would like to shift either ratio (self-talk or talk about others) to be more positive. If so, experiment with it for the rest of the week.

    *   For self-talk about yourself, the first step is to make a list of all your positive qualities, successes, and aspirations. Read

over the list daily and add to it. During the week, be on the lookout for occasions when you demonstrate one or more of your positive attributes. When you catch yourself in a positive moment, be generous with your silent self-congratulation. You'll probably sound stilted to yourself at first. Everyone does. Take it slow, and learn to appreciate self-appreciation. See if your self-talk ratio becomes more positive.

- For talk about others, be on the lookout for positive acts that people do, either directly toward you, or that you observe. Also note characteristics about others that you enjoy or find pleasing. Each time you catch someone in a positive act, or find something pleasing about the person, make a silent statement to yourself about that. If you like, consider making a written notation when it's convenient. Keep a journal this week about others' positive acts and positive characteristics. Also, at the end of each day, list as many acts and characteristics as you can recall having spotted that day. See how many you can come up with. Then review the pattern in your observations and journaling this week. See if the journaling grows in length and in the range of entries. Also see how your ratio of positive-to-negative talk about others shifts.

3. In one month, repeat this exercise for either type of self-talk. Put it in your calendar in advance. Repeat monthly.

4. You don't have to wait for a whole month to readminister this practice. Repeat it whenever you feel the need for a good talking-to.

Chapter 20:
Telephone Meditation:
A Mindfulness Practice

*F*or the last few days, I've found myself thinking a lot about telephone meditation. It's been dancing around in my mind lately, so I'm going to follow the scent and see where it leads.

Telephone meditation is a mindfulness practice created by Thich Nhat Hanh, the wise and beloved Vietnamese Buddhist monk whose retreat center, Plum Village (www.plumvillage.org), is thriving in France. *Thay* (pronounced Tie, which is Vietnamese for teacher, and is how he's known to the many thousands who have been in his presence) has created a raft of such practices to help facilitate the art of mindful living. Before describing my own experiences with telephone meditation, let's hear about it in Thay's own words, taken from a dharma talk you can read in its entirety on the Internet (www.sinc.sunysb.edu/Clubs/buddhism/dailylife/thayq-a.html).

> And when you hear the telephone ringing you can consider it to be the sound of the mindfulness bell. You practice telephone meditation. Every time you hear the telephone ringing you stay exactly where you are (laughter). You breathe in and breathe out and enjoy your breathing. Listen, listen—this wonderful sound brings you back to your true home. Then when you

hear the second ring you stand up and you go to the telephone with dignity.

I hope this snippet conveys something of the profound gentleness, clarity, and wisdom of this remarkable man of peace, who is still going full tilt in his eighties. He seems to have updated his telephone meditation practice to keep up with technology. When I learned this practice from him fourteen years ago, he taught us to wait until after the third ring. Apparently, someone's told him about voice mail systems, many of which are triggered during the third ring, and he's made the adjustment. Thay is timeless, but he keeps up with the times.

Instead of grabbing the receiver on the first ring (or pressing the speaker button on the console) and barking "Hello!" or "Yes?" you simply let the phone ring. You watch your breath and come home to yourself—the self you have lost sight of by getting caught up in your activity of the moment. During the first ring, don't check e-mails, don't clip that nasty cuticle, and don't open that interoffice envelope staring up at you. Instead, follow your breath as it comes in, and follow it as it exits your body. Repeat the same pattern on the second ring: one breath in, one breath out. As Thay does in the quotation above, you might say a *gatha* (pronounced gah-ta): a short, prayerful expression, such as "Listen, listen—this wonderful sound brings me back to my true home." Another gatha I learned from him is this: "May this conversation be for the benefit of all beings." If that's too large a sentiment for you, then try "May we find common ground." Or make up your own. As the teenagers say these days, it's all good.

Here's an interesting wrinkle: smile as you pick up the receiver. In fact, smile as you reach for the receiver in the first place. You may well be wondering, "Now why would I want to smile at a telephone?" Here's why. The 297 muscles (really, 297 of them) involved in creating our smile tell the brain that we're happy, and the message gets transmitted to the caller as we issue our smiley greeting. The caller senses the smile in our voice. You see, our brains don't know that we're deliberately making our faces smile. As brilliant as it is about so many things, the brain can't distinguish whether (a) something external has made you happy, (b) you're putting on a smile because you think it's a good mindfulness practice, or (c) you're overmedicated. All it knows is "Alert! Smile detected down below! Apparently, I am happy!" And you place the caller in a better frame of mind because, instead of barking or droning our greeting, you've sonically caressed the person on the other end of the line.

Try it for yourself. The caller may think you're on something, that maybe you've increased your meds. But—and here's the point—the person will truly like it, despite what he might think or say! And it will launch the conversation in such a sweet way that things almost inevitably go better because of it. Case in point: After I handwrote part of the draft of this chapter, my phone rang. I practiced telephone meditation. I let the first two rings go by, followed my breath, and smiled and picked up the receiver before the third ring. Darned if it didn't work! I felt so calm, so eager to hear the caller's voice. I truly believe it got us off to a great start. Interesting side note: my client on the other end of the phone began the conversation with, "Hi, Ed. I've been thinking a lot about meditation lately." This completely blew me away! As my grandmother would have said, go figure.

I don't do telephone meditation often enough for my own well-being, and that of my callers. It's often said in education circles that you teach a subject in order to learn it. Maybe that's why I've been driven to write about this topic: to come home to myself, as Thay phrases it, by coming home to telephone meditation and other mindfulness practices that I've let languish. And coming home to oneself is a phrase that has such meaning for me that it forms a core element of my work: to bring people home to themselves. I can't very well do that if I'm not at home in myself, can I?

One practice I do more often is walking meditation. When walking from point A to point B, I do it mindfully (as often as I can remind myself about being mindful). I hope you'll try it too. There's a catch, however. There's a natural tendency to do walking meditation so slowly that you'll appear to onlookers as though you're in a trance. So, you'll want to be careful about where you do your mindful walking. If you're in public, go at your normal walking pace so you don't become labeled, and so a police cruiser doesn't sound its siren and pull over to question you. If you're in private, go at your most mindful pace. Either way, try it.

The point is to come home to yourself, using whatever means works for you. Plan to get home to yourself more often. It will benefit not only you, but also everyone you encounter—even telemarketers! You see, the deep ease you exude when you're at home in yourself will be contagious for other people, and they will interact with you and others in a more spacious manner. It's an example of a virtuous cycle. And because what goes around comes around, it will come back around to you. It works that way.

Practice

1. To get a handle on what practices bring you home to yourself, answer these questions:

    - What does *home* feel like to you?

    - Is it a location in the body? If so, where?

    - Is it a vaguely-felt sense?

    - Or is it something else?

- Who are you with, when you are feeling at home?

  Chances are, the people you're with at those times constitute home to you. That's important information to have.

2. Here's another way to find out where, and what, home is for you. Pay attention to times when you simply sink into wherever you are and find yourself uttering (or just feeling internally a sense of), *Ahhhh*, or your equivalent sound of deep calm. That's probably home for you.

   - Pay careful attention to how it feels in your body, the emotions you're having, and what your mind is doing.

   - Pay attention to what (and who) is around you as you're experiencing this sense of home.

   - Savor it!

Chapter 21:
Meditation:
It's Not Just for Telephones
Anymore

$\mathcal{M}$y friend Jim Blankenheim e-mailed me in response to the piece on telephone meditation, to broaden my horizons. That's Jim's job: broadening my horizons. Most everything he says stretches me, gives me a chuckle, or does both. Here's what he wrote:

> It's been hard (so far) to break into a new habit of telephone meditation. Working on it, though, and when I remember to stop and 'center' before flipping open the cell, it works. Here's a new idea ... I'm going to try the same technique before "opening" certain e-mails. You know, the ones from difficult clients, etc. I guess the technique would work with instant messaging too. I'll let you know how it's working.

Jim's thoughts about cell-phone and e-mail meditation gave me a case of indented forehead syndrome (IFS). You know, when someone says something so brilliant (and, in retrospect, so incredibly obvious) that you smack your forehead with the heel of your hand. Of course! Why hadn't I seen it before, and why hadn't I included it in that piece? The answers, obviously, are (a) that's what I have Jim for; it's his job, and (b) that's what future writing is for. To honor his contribution, I hereby designate cell-phone and e-mail opening meditation as Blankenheimlich Maneuvers.

As I thought further about Jim's message, it made me realize that we can use almost any stimulus—not just phone calls and e-mails—as occasions for awakening. All we have to do are the following five steps:

1. Create an intention to be awake and mindful in the present moment, to take it all in. In the words of Caribou Coffee's ^{TM} slogan, "Life Is short, Stay awake for it."

2. Find practices that help us to be mindful and awake. These ways are as plentiful as our imaginations and our senses allow.

3. Experiment playfully with those practices and create our own; what works for me won't necessarily work for you, and vice versa. And what works for me today won't necessarily work for me two weeks from now. Things change, as I imagine you've noticed.

4. Remember to *do* the practices. (That's why they're called *practices.)*

5. Be kind and gentle with ourselves when we forget to remember.

If you're looking to develop some cues (what Thich Nhat Hanh calls "bells of awakening") to help you come home to yourself, here are three guidelines:

•   Pick something that happens frequently, or that you do frequently. Select something that's at least neutral for you or, preferably, that has a positive charge. That's why so many forms of meditation focus on the breath. For most of us, the breath is blessedly easy, regular, and frequent. And it can be savory, as we discover, the more we do breath-centered meditation. It's also why basketball players typically take a deep breath just before shooting free throws during a game. It sloughs off tension and overstimulation, promotes focusing, and centers them. *Swish!*

- Pick something that you have a good chance of remembering to do, and can do reasonably well and without distraction. (You don't want to be evaluating or censoring yourself as you do the exercise, and you don't want distracting sounds to divert you.) Remembering to breathe into two rings of the telephone—doable. Remembering to breathe twice before comforting a screaming infant—probably not.

- Build in a continual positive feedback loop when you remember to practice the practice. For example, after doing the Blankenheimlich Maneuver before reading an e-mail, smile to yourself and say a quiet *yes* (or say, "Jim would be so proud."). When you neglect to practice or you perform it poorly, instead of berating yourself, do what a toddler does when falling down. Pick yourself up and continue toddling, undaunted.

One of the wonderful benefits of writing about this topic is that I get to reflect on how it applies in my own life. I realize that I use a few bells of awakening that work for me, to a greater or lesser extent. Sharing mine with you may stimulate the search for your own.

Telephone Meditation: I don't use it often enough (maybe 25 to 30 percent of the time), but when I do, it always comes up a winner.

Staircase Meditation: Thich Nhat Hanh says that he has made a contract with himself regarding staircases. He pledged, some twenty-five years ago, to use stair-climbing as a meditative occasion, and he says he's never broken this pledge. In our Madison home, we are blessed with a wonderfully wide and spacious staircase. It's ideal for walking meditation, and at the landing, it's perfect for Pause-and-Breathe Meditation. I'm good for about a 20 percent frequency on this. Staircase meditation is an available, easy, and restorative practice. Now I need to ask myself my favorite appreciative question: what would it take for me to do it more often?

Too-darned-slow-internet-connection Meditation: a variant of the Blankenheimlich Maneuver. I've learned to make a virtue of necessity. I've treated the occasionally lengthy Internet start-up time or lost e-mail message as an opportunity to breathe and center myself: *Ahhhh.* I'm up to about 50 or 60 percent on this practice. It's one of my favorite practices because, with Internet speeds being so variable and computers being so ornery, there's no shortage of occasions to practice. Also because it's a great antidote for my default habit, which is to gnash my teeth in anguish and feel intensely annoyed. *Ahhhh* is so much better than *Arghhhh!*

Dishwasher-emptying Meditation: When I am not in a rush to do something else or be somewhere else, I actually enjoy the ritual of emptying the dishwasher. I like to mindfully stack the plates as quietly as the crockery will allow and as high as I dare, mindfully carry them over to the cupboard (all the while enjoying the sense of mild danger that accompanies the prospect of dropping every last one of them: a safer, though milder, thrill than skydiving), and place each stack as quietly and precisely as I can on the shelves. This one is a biggie for me. I'm up to 90 or 100 percent on it. It's a nice example of making a virtue of necessity. These days, I actually look forward to doing it! (I'm not sure how wise it is to go on record about it, for fear that it will be construed in my household as a public commitment to my family.)

Hotel-room-departure Meditation: Since I have had more occasions to travel, I have found it centering and practical to stop, breathe, and scan the room with fresh eyes just before leaving a hotel to get to the airport. The drill is something like this: Have I taken everything? Have I checked the closet? The bathroom? The bureau drawers? Have I left a tip for the housekeeper? This ritual probably takes no more than fifteen extra seconds, and it has two outstanding results: one, when I leave the room, I'm more relaxed and cheerful, and two, it's reduced the number of things I leave behind to an average of 1.3 per trip. I do this practice about 80 percent of the time, sometimes with a greater and sometimes with a lesser degree of mindfulness and completeness. If anyone finds an almost-new black topcoat with a gray zip-in liner, please let me know.

I wonder what your bells of awakening are. And how you discovered them, and how you have benefited from using them. And what you have done with my topcoat.

Practice

1. Think about your favorite practices for becoming more mindful and centered.

   - For those practices that work best for you, give thanks.

   - Create a conscious intention to continue or even to expand their use. Decide when you will put them to use. Put them to use and observe how they work.

2. Create a new appreciative meditation practice for yourself. To do so, use the guidelines mentioned in the chapter. Think about actions or events that

    - occur frequently;
    - have a positive charge for you;
    - you can remember to do;
    - you can do reasonably well.

      When you try out your new practice, remember to build in a positive feedback loop. Give yourself verbal praise. I am told that chocolate also works well.

Chapter 22:
Why Am I Here Today?

*I*t's wonderful how one thing leads to the next. (When you think about it, we'd be in a real fix if it didn't.) Like, for example, how my piece on telephone meditation (chapter 20) led to my friend Jim's reply detailing his innovative use of cell-phone-opening meditation, which led me to the next piece, on other bells of awakening (chapter 21).

It is here that the plot thickens. The weekend I sent out the latter column, I made a presentation at the Financial Planning Association (FPA) convention in Nashville. My handler was Stephanie Bogan, whom I'd never met before. Stephanie's job was to make sure I had what I needed, distribute handouts, introduce me, and ensure that I ended precisely at 5:15. You'll be glad to learn that she performed flawlessly. And why shouldn't she? She's the owner of a successful consulting firm (www.quantuvis.com) whose mission includes "To help our clients improve their performance and achieve their potential." Thank you, Stephanie. You helped. I improved. I achieved.

She gave me a business card so I could put her on the list for the columns. Almost immediately, I received a wonderful, wise, and instructive reply to the most recent column on other bells of awakening. I found her message so cogent, and found myself drinking it in so eagerly, that I asked her for permission to cite it here. She readily agreed. Here's what she wrote:

A wise client of mine taught me something valuable many years ago. I admit I'm most often remiss in doing it, but have found an electronic substitute to remind me. Here goes: When Lew (the wise client) starts his day at work, the first thing he does, before opening e-mail, checking messages, or looking at the in-box, he sits down squarely in his chair, places both palms flat on the desk, takes a deep breath, and asks, "Why am I here today?" Most assuredly the answer isn't to respond to the e-mail or move the paper from one in-box to another, but to have some impact on those with whom and for whom he works.

We've institutionalized this practice to help everyone on our team remember this. We're religious users of GoldMine, so the first item on our calendar at 7:45 each morning is *Why Are You Here Today*—and in the notes "To help our clients improve their performance and achieve their potential." It's also the first item on our daily meeting agenda. As a result, I'm focused on the purpose of my work, not on the work itself.

Being a business owner, like many I can get focused on work and not let it go, so at the end of my day there is another reminder end-of-day ritual. In my notes, it asks how I did today, did I focus on the important things, what can I learn from today, and then says … now let it go and go home! This is quite effective at helping me leave work at work so I can enjoy the real blessings in my life at home. Thanks for your insight. I'm going to try your suggestions as well. I can benefit from a more relaxed pace in my spirit, even when I'm working fast and hard. I think everyone can.

Isn't this terrific? Stephanie has extended Lew's practice to achieve an end-of-workday closure: a truly elegant innovation. I sent this chapter to Stephanie in advance, and asked her who Lew was. She replied that he was her mentor. I asked her to clarify because I thought she'd referred to him as a client. Here's what she e-mailed back: "He was a client, but his wisdom made him a mentor." Clearly, she has a touch of the poet in her, and more than a touch of the profound.

"Why am I here today?" If that question isn't a bell of awakening, I don't know what is. As with other bells, its job is to orient us to what truly matters, and to enable us to filter out the rest. Asking, "Why am I here today?"—or arranging for our computers to ask us that question—grabs us and forces us to look beyond the mental cobwebs, the tactics, and the facts of the case, and to zero in on the core.

It makes me wonder why *I* am here today. Why I am writing this chapter, why I am writing this book. Many reasons suggest themselves: To teach. To learn more about what I'm seeking to teach. To get my name and ideas out there. To attract more business. For each of these reasons, I could ask myself the *why* question, and then answer again, ask it again, and so on. I'd follow the trail, hoping to get to the core reason I'm writing this stuff. But I don't need to do that because my mind has quickly jumped to endgame. I realize that I write it because I can, and because I must.

I truly love writing these pieces. I love the organic way that one piece leads to the next. At one time, I was a member of a writing group for a period of years. I loved its support and regularity, and I loved how it nurtured the development of my writing style. I've missed it. And in the process of writing the columns, and now this book, my readers and I have created a virtuous cycle, in which we stretch each other. I've increasingly surrendered to this process, and I allow whatever bizarre-sounding associations emerge to guide me. The sequence of chapters, beginning with telephone meditation, proceeding to the piece triggered by Jim's e-mail, and culminating in this chapter, is a good case in point.

My experience is akin to novelists who realize they can't control their characters. The writer awakens every day, sits down at the desk, waits (in the words of one writer who said it best) "to learn what the damn characters are going to do today," and then writes it down. Many writers maintain that they're just taking dictation. It's like that for me.

My engagement with readers and with the writing process makes me feel more alive and vibrant. It brings back the elevator speech which I created several years ago in a session I attended on elevator speeches. (In business parlance, an elevator speech is a brief, vivid statement of what you do and the value it brings. It's designed to be delivered in the time span of a short elevator ride.) Here's what I wrote, in that session: "I bring all of myself to my work, so we may bring all of your *self* to life." I feel that I'm bringing all of myself to this writing. And so, I write these pieces because I can … and because I must. If I didn't, I'd get out of tune. My mental and emotional machinery wouldn't work quite as well. It's kind of like my stepson, who, if he doesn't strum his guitar a little each night, gets out of kilter. He knows what he needs to do, and he makes sure he does it—a sure sign of robust mental health.

I invite you to ask yourself Stephanie's question: "why am I here today?" It may be a good time to hit the Refresh button on your purpose for showing up. You might ask yourself her compelling question and think about your own elevator speech, your mission statement, or other relevant answers. Follow the scent. Keep asking *why* after each answer. Get to the core of it.

I hope that your core answer utilizes all your gifts. I hope you do what you do because you can … and because you must. You need that for optimal health and vibrancy. The world needs it from you as well. This beautiful and beleaguered planet needs every person's help, the full expression of all our gifts. Isn't that why we're here today?

Practice

1. Following Stephanie's lead, create a screen saver for your computer, a Post-it Note™ for your calendar, or another bell of awakening to remind you at the beginning of your day to ask, "Why am I here?" Make your answer to that question bigger than "To check off items on my to-do list."

2. Make the following practice into a mini-project for your work group. Apply practice 1 with your group, to verify why the group exists, and to create visible reminders of that purpose. Then, over the next couple of weeks, notice if its answer to the purpose question begins to permeate its conversations.

3. Bring your workday to closure with an end-of-day shutdown. Answer the following questions, or create your own, before you leave your workplace.

   - When did you focus on what's most important today?
   - What's the best thing you did today for clients? For colleagues? For yourself?
   - What did you learn today that was important?

Chapter 23:
How Can I Make You Happy Today?

*A*s I handwrote the title of this chapter, I experienced a surge of energy. I felt it in my heart and my face, and I heard my inner voice say, "Don't you just love that question?"

In case you hear yourself saying, "Well … actually, no, I don't," let me share how I happened upon it. It's not original with me. It came from the mouth of Dan, who is an original.

Dan, proprietor of Dan's Limo Service, met me at Logan Airport in Boston last Thursday afternoon to drive me to the Courtyard by Marriott™ in Waltham, prior to a workshop I was to deliver the next day. It's hard not to like someone who has a smile, positive energy, enthusiasm, and good cheer … all of which was communicated just in his voice! Dan demonstrated all of that on the phone, as we arranged the logistics of the pickup, and he was everything in person that his phone persona promised.

I should mention that I have a thing for limo and cab drivers: I love hearing their stories, getting to know them through these stories, and being impressed and moved by the courage, resilience, and heroism that they have summoned in order to emigrate from the Sudan, Lithuania, Kazakhstan, or any of the myriad other foreign lands that supply much of our labor pool these days. I can't remember the last time I met a cab driver from (I mean, really *from*) Philadelphia. I'm sure they're still around somewhere. Maybe in Denver.

I asked Dan where he was from. Given the awful tension, bordering on cultural paranoia, that surrounds anyone vaguely foreign these days (especially if they are "not like us"), I have learned not to jump in and bluntly ask, "Where are you from?" I'm fearful the driver will clam up because of his fear that I'm out to inspect his papers. With Dan, as with others, I wait until there's the beginning of a back-and-forth between us. I pick my moment, when it feels safe and appropriate, and I quietly say, "May I ask where you're from?" That question always seems to be received as an invitation to tell one's story. Dan was no different in that regard.

"My father was from Ethiopia, and my mother from Cuba," he said, pronouncing it Coo-bah. I wondered silently where his parents would have met. He proceeded to give me his provenance, as one would a piece of art, a painting, or a bottle of wine. Born in East Berlin, moved to West Berlin at age six ("three days before Kennedy said, 'Ich bin ein Berliner'"), grew up there, spent time living in Italy and Switzerland, and had been here for the last thirty-three years. "I never was to Coo-bah yet. Have to wait for Castro to die." I quickly learned that he had "six boys: two in college, two graduating from high school, and two seven-year-olds. Two sets of twins!" I was mesmerized by his story, his charm, his life force. I was like Renée Zellweger's character in *Jerry Maguire*. Dan had me from hello.

The ride to Waltham, and Dan's ongoing recitation, was punctuated by a series of calls on his cell phone. His limo, after all, was his office. He had the cell phone's speaker on, and I could tell that (a) each caller was a woman, and (b) he made each one feel absolutely special: familiar and important to him, caressed by his warmth, charm, and affection, and by a wide-open embrace of her and of life. Some callers were executives; some were executive assistants. All got his total attention, and all received the *Dan treatment*. They quickly completed their arrangements, and he bade each a warm farewell. After about the fourth iteration, I commented, "Dan, you certainly have a way of romancing your women callers." Again, Dan didn't disappoint. Letting nary a millisecond pass, he said with a laugh that was more of an outburst, "How do you think I got six boys?!" A great retort with, I imagine, more than a hint of truth in it.

We soon got to the Courtyard, and after exchanging cash for a receipt, he unloaded my bags, wheeled them into the lobby, and deposited them at the front desk—a courtly gentleman, and I didn't need to be a woman to receive his treatment. We arranged a Saturday morning return ride to Logan. I must say, I got a real high from the whole experience. The "romance of the road" soon pales for consultants, public speakers, and workshop facilitators. An encounter with a Dan provides us a genuine lift. The mood persisted for hours. Also, I'm sure it set in motion a virtuous cycle. I was eager to share my story with my wife, especially because of Dan's lineage. You see, my stepson is Ethiopian American and is interested in and proud of all things Ethiopian. Also, I was and eager to transport the story of Dan into the workshop. I found a perfect place for it, in speaking about the appreciative space created when one practices appreciation: a space that invites us in, and makes us feel fully received and positively regarded. Dan is a master appreciator.

I was able to contrast Dan and his appreciative space with the cab driver who took me on Friday morning to Bentley College for the workshop. I knew I was in for a different ride when, in the confusion about whether I was his fare, he asked, "Did they tell you at the front desk that they called a cab or their courtesy van?" When I said I had no idea, he replied with an anguished scowl, "Why am I not surprised?" Now, I should say that we did talk about lots of subjects en route. And that he was from the Boston area. That much was detectable. Somehow, each subject we broached came back around to being about him: about how he was beleaguered by this big-box store (you know the one, with the yellow price tag on the front) or that politician, or something or someone else. I was grateful and appreciative that he clearly knew which building to deposit me in front of, and that he was cordial, even funny, in his acrid way. Mostly I was relieved and glad to get where I needed to be, and on time, and positively excited by the impending workshop. Which was wonderful, by the way: great folks, great times, great learning for us all. To be sure, I was not uplifted by the second driver as I had been with Dan. I did, however, find the encounter with him to be a useful counterpoint, in my own mind and in the workshop, to the story of Dan.

The title of this chapter is a direct quote from Dan. It was his way of answering the phone on at least two of the calls I overheard. I could hardly believe my ears when I first heard him issue this greeting: "Hello, this is Dan. How can I make you happy today?" And this was before he knew who was calling. "What if it had been a bill collector or a telemarketer?" I wondered. "What would that person think?" When I talk about Appreciative Inquiry, I characterize appreciative questions as being invitations. Dan's greeting was the perfect example of one such invitation: "How can I make you happy today?" is, as the Master Card™ commercial says, priceless.

What a wonderful way to embrace the world! What marvels, I wondered, could I give rise to if I created an appreciative space with my wife by asking her that question (or by silently inhabiting the question, without even asking it)? What about with others? With myself? I pondered one more question: what would it take to create the inner space from which I could issue that invitation?

I'm still working at it. As the poet Rilke wrote in *Letters to a Young Poet*, "Try to love the questions themselves, as if they were locked rooms or books written in a very foreign language. Don't search for the answers, which could not be given to you now, because you would not be able to live them. And the point is to live everything. Live the questions now. Perhaps then, someday far in the future, you will gradually, without even noticing it, live your way into the answer."

I'm living the questions.

To resume and conclude the story of Dan, he picked me up at the Courtyard at 7:33 AM on Saturday, precisely as I was stepping out the door with my bags, and he greeted me like an old friend. (No, he didn't ask me how he could make me happy today. I imagine he knew the answer: by getting me to the airport in plenty of time for my 9:05 AM flight.)

When we got in the cab, I commented on what a classically beautiful New England fall morning it was. He responded in kind, calling it (several times, for emphasis) "a gorgeous day." He had a way of prolonging the first syllable of "gorgeous," as though he were sweeping his hand across the vista before us, and then uttering the second syllable as his hand dropped to his side: *gorrr-geous*. He then provided a litany of the day's bounty, including how God surely loves the United States, because He lets all His children come here and find ways to live in harmony. Surely Dan is an innocent, or he has not been exposed to the darker forces of our society. However, this didn't diminish my delight in his company or my love of his positive energy and his bountiful, loving nature. I probably wouldn't retain him as my political campaign manager, but then again, I'm not running for anything (except the airport).

I must tell you how we closed the book, at least on this trip. As I bade him farewell in front of the Northwest Airlines terminal, and he opened his door to get back in the limo, he said, "Have a peaceful day." I was so moved. It was such a perfect way to take our leave. It was so very Dan. I tell you, he had me at good-bye.

Practice

1. Be aware of (a) situations where you feel joy, happiness, peacefulness, excitement, humor, or other pleasurable feelings, and (b) people who make you feel those ways. Savor the feelings by luxuriating in the experiences while they last. Feel gratitude for the situation, the people, and the feelings they elicit.

    - Ask yourself what about the situation and/or the person producing these wonderful feelings. Getting clarity about those characteristics will help you with the practice in the next bullet point.

    - Consider what you can do to place yourself in those situations more often. When you have the answers, act on them.

2. Be alert to people and situations that are downers for you—occasions when you feel boredom, anger, humiliation, discouragement, or other unpleasant feelings.

    Answer the following three questions:

    - What about these people and situations produces the negative feelings?

    - What can you do to turn these circumstances in a positive direction?

    - If, realistically, there is little you can do to turn around those circumstances, is there a way to avoid them altogether? (If not, the next question is, What can you do to minimize their negative effects on you?)

Chapter 24:
Toll Collectors with
More Than a Smile

*T*here we were, the three of us, motoring back to Denver's ultra-modern airport located in the middle of nowhere. We were coming from a wonderful financial life planning conference at the YMCA of the Rockies, in beautiful Estes Park.

Phil, who was driving, looked on in amazement as the toll collector, a blond woman somewhere in her middle years, greeted him with a generous smile and said, "Hi, how are ya? That'll be two dollars, please." She gave him a "Thank you," along with the smile on her face and in her voice, as he handed her the two bills.

Phil and Eric, who was riding shotgun in front of me, couldn't believe their eyes and ears. Phil blurted out with a startle, "Did you hear that?!"—much as he might have responded to sudden gunfire heard in his West Point days. "She actually thanked me!" Then it was Eric's turn to express amazement. He said, in his delightful North Carolina accent, "I sure as heck never heard that on the New Jersey Turnpike!"

I wasn't too surprised myself because, despite having grown up in Brooklyn, I'd grown used to the Midwestern politeness of Illinois toll takers on rural stretches of I-90. Nonetheless, I laughed at Eric's contrasting our appreciative toll collector with her New Jersey counterparts. After all, a large part of humor is the unexpected pairing of incompatible elements, and Eric had nailed it perfectly. Continuing in the vein he'd established, I wondered aloud how the supervisor of a New Jersey Turnpike toll collector would respond if he (and you can be sure it would be a he) overheard one of his toll collectors greeting a driver as our Colorado version had greeted Phil. Once again, and without missing a beat, Eric nailed it: "One more like that, and you're out!" We all had a hearty laugh at that ridiculous scene, worthy of Jon Stewart.

As I write these words, I relive the scene all over again, with a smile on my face. It's delicious for me, for many reasons. For one thing, its pure comedic foolishness. It's funny, even more so because Eric's gorgeous drawl made him the least likely and most effective commentator. And I smile because of the genuine affection and ease among the three of us, united by a shared commitment to helping people find and lead their hearts' core life—and having had that commitment reaffirmed and deepened through the great conference we'd just attended. And for me, the smile brightens further as I remember Phil calling her the appreciative toll collector. It's a funny concept, and a great one, made better because it meant that Phil grasped what my two conference sessions were about. I'm encouraged when people catch the appreciation virus that I'm deliberately spreading. Both he and Eric had definitely caught it.

I laughed once again at Eric's statement and said, "You know, I think I can get a column out of that." Not long afterward, we pulled up to the second and final I-470 tollbooth before the airport. Wouldn't you know it, we got the exact same treatment from our second appreciative toll taker! No sooner had Phil closed his window than both of them said, "Another one! Did you hear that?" I can't say that it made our day, because we were already having a pretty good one, but it made it brighter and even more special.

In the subsequent two days, I had a lot of thoughts about that whole event: how much fun it was; how much the three of us appreciated these two women's open and generous greetings; how awful it must be to be trapped all day inside a metal cage on a New Jersey highway, breathing in toxic fumes and processing hundreds of cars per hour; and how our two appreciative Coloradans have the wide open skies and the flat scrubland as their vista. And I wondered what it would take (or whether it was possible at all) to make that New Jersey tollbooth into an appreciative space, and about whether all this focus on appreciation is easy for me to say. (The answer to that last one is "Yes, it is"—because my life is far easier, and perhaps richer, than many others'.)

I'd planned to explore some of those thoughts in this piece. But what strikes me about the whole episode is its *aloha* quality. *Aloha,* according to George Kinder, is an Hawaiian term that means the passing of a blessing from one person to another, without regard for economic differences. That's a very different meaning from the one we ordinarily associate with *aloha,* and George believes that an *aloha* sensibility is the highest stage of spiritual development. (I heartily recommend his book, *The Seven Stages of Money Maturity.* It forms one of the pillars of the Kinder Institute of Life Planning, whose conference we'd just attended.)

I marvel at how these two women seemed to believe that their jobs weren't just collecting tolls. In fact, I fancied that perhaps they conceived of their toll-taking jobs as a ruse, a devious means of passing blessings all day. It's akin to passing out spiritual handbills to frantic passersby in Grand Central Station at rush hour. And I marvel at how, by Phil's returning the smile and offering his hearty "You're welcome!" to each, he was passing a blessing back to them. I marvel further at the rich potential for *aloha* that each day, and each moment, brings: a simple hello, the preparing and serving of a meal, the giving of a presentation, the applause at the end, the gracious acknowledgement of a family member or colleague's doing his job, whatever that job is. All these are blessings. All are *aloha*. (I'm reminded of Aman, who always blesses Jody for his dinner by thanking her at the end: "Thanks for the food, Mom. It was *really* good." For some unaccountable reason, I don't get the same treatment when I cook. Am I missing something here?)

The operative word here is the potential for an act to be *aloha*. Here's what it takes to transform an ordinary act into *aloha*.

- A recognition of the potential for ordinary and routine acts to become exalted, and even sacred

- The intention—an intention of the heart, more than the mind—to transform an act into a blessing

- Being aware and present, in the millisecond before the act, so that we can act on the heart's core intention to confer *aloha*.

And we must be equally present, by the way, to be on the receiving end of *aloha*. The very acceptance of a blessing is itself the conferring of a blessing in return. It says, "I recognize what you did as *aloha*, I thank you, and I don't take it for granted; I take it as granted." Thomas Merton, the American Benedictine monk, said that if we could see the beauty of each others' true natures, the problem is that we would spend all our time bowing. I think that bowing to each other is a wonderful use of our time and energy.

Here is a quotation from Dr. Martin Luther King, Jr., on a sign above the door in the conference dining room at the Estes Park YMCA: 'Everyone can be great, because everyone can serve." And everyone can bow in *aloha*.

Practice

It is sometimes said that the greatest gift we can give another is our presence. I take that to mean our truly showing up when we show up.

Select several routine activities that you typically perform on auto-pilot. For the next seven days, truly show up when you do them. Here are some examples that may apply. Identify others of your own. Do them with conscious intent, and observe what happens.

- When you greet someone, instead of asking, "How are you?" ask, "What's been the best part of your day so far?" Pause and really listen to the answers. Let what the person is saying sink in.

- When someone gives you something (a report, a cup of coffee, a package, etc.), consider that she is not just doing her job, but giving you a gift as well. Respond accordingly to the gift, and to the gift-giver.

- When you climb into your car, look around and appreciate the many ways in which it supports you, and what it makes possible for you. Once you have done that, start the car.

- When someone asks you, "Got a minute?" say "Sure!" Give the person as much time as he needs. Keep your hand from reaching for the doorknob, and your eyes from wandering toward the clock. Be completely present with him. That's a big *aloha*.

At the end of each day, spend a moment reflecting on how you applied the intention to be present and confer *aloha*, and what happened as a result. At the end of a full seven days, reflect on what you have learned during this past week about being present, and about the gifts that flow from it (gifts to others, as well as those that flow back to you).

Chapter 25:
Stop the World

The world is too much with us is the title of a William Wordsworth sonnet that lodged in my brain while I was a student at Midwood High School in Brooklyn eons ago. The title reemerged just now, as I was thinking about how busy our minds are so much of the time. (Mine is, anyway. It's like the Roller Derby in there sometimes.) Our minds and our entire lives can get so busy that we have trouble slowing down and letting our lives speak to us: our needs, desires, and longings; the voices within us that want expression; the life within us that is bursting to be released. Even the pharmaceutical ads understand this. One of them is now telling us, "Your dreams miss you."

Many of us keep ourselves super busy, habitually surrounding ourselves with a world too much with us, to avoid the complications that would ensue if we dared give voice to our longings. As for the rest of us, we don't mean to drown ourselves in client work, carpools, exercise class, e-mail addictions, and the like, but we've somehow lost our way, and we don't know how to stop the proceedings of our lives. Can you relate?

Dr. David Kundtz can. He's written an entire book on stopping. It's called, oddly enough, *Stopping*. (Its subtitle is *How to Be Still When You Have to Keep Going*.) He speaks of three kinds of stopping, each with a different time frame and with different practices:

Stillpoints: These are short interludes that we can build into our lives, as mini-respites or breathers that fortify us for the next activity. Allowing two minutes (or even fifteen, as some people do) between appointments, to replenish ourselves, is a perfect stillpoint. These mini-respites are not to be used to cram in a quick e-mail check, return that beckoning phone message, or have a mini-conference with your associate. These times are for you, not for getting one more thing done. Meditation (including telephone meditation, which I've discussed in prior chapters) is another great stillpoint practice. So is gazing out the window and letting your mind rest, especially if the view is tranquil and calming.

Stopovers: These are longer stoppings that can be for an hour, or as much as a couple of days. A walk in the woods or sitting in a park and watching kids at play are dandy stopovers. Thanksgiving weekend, if it's not programmed with activities, is a wonderful stopover opportunity. I recently improvised a variation. It's called taking-a-whole-lot-of-stuff-home-from-the-office-on-Wednesday-of-Thanksgiving-week ... and-never-looking-at-a-blessed-piece-of-it-all-weekend. It was very effective and had no guilt-inducing side effects. The briefer stillpoints, while necessary, are not sufficient. Stopovers are vital for most of us, on a regular basis. Perhaps that's why weekend getaways have become so popular and, for many of us, so necessary.

Grinding Halts: These are the stop-the-world ... I-want-to-get-off kinds of emergency brakes that we may need to activate once, twice, or perhaps three times in an average lifetime. A grinding halt can last a month or perhaps six weeks in duration, according to Kundtz. It's truly a retreat from our usual, overburdening routines, and is often triggered by a life transition or crisis. For nineteenth and early twentieth-century upper-class people, having a so-called nervous breakdown was a socially approved way of taking a grinding halt. Few of us have that luxury, so we may need to do some careful planning in order to have our time away.

I speak from personal experience. Back in 1997, I was sorely in need of stopping the careening-to-nowhere that typified my unhappy and overwrought life at that time. My work was unrewarding, and there were heaping gobs of it. I felt unloved and isolated in my community. I was perpetually lonely, and I felt as though my spirit were wasting away. As the Alcoholics Anonymous people say, I was sick and tired of being sick and tired. My career coach at the time finally said, "Look, I've never told anyone that they needed to take a leave of absence from their work, but I'm telling you that now! You're burned out, and you need to get away." (Thank you, Linda.)

I felt like I'd been hammered by a Muhammad Ali right hook, but as my head hit the canvas (metaphorically, fortunately), I heard an inner voice say, "Cool, I can go to Plum Village!" I successfully negotiated a four-month leave (unpaid, sad to say) from KPMG Peat Marwick and gleefully planned a two-week trip to France to visit Plum Village (www.plumvillage.org), the home and retreat center of Thich Nhat Hanh.

Two great things happened in the ensuing period. The first is that I became acquainted with Appreciative Inquiry at a national conference just a few weeks before beginning my leave. The second is that I went to Plum Village for two weeks ... and stayed for thirteen. I was there for the entire winter retreat, which consumed virtually my entire leave of absence (or, as I came to call it, my leave of my senses).

This was way more than a grinding halt. I'm not sure I have the right term for it, but it sure was necessary. I had been in critical condition and needed extreme intervention. To this day, I experience undiminished gratitude for having been able to take such a deep and joyous plunge in my life. I know that few of us have the freedom to take that leave, and to follow it up with a year off. It was late in the retreat when I realized I was going to quit my job upon my return to America. I didn't make a conscious decision to quit. It was more as if I experienced a public service announcement from my unconscious mind and heart. It said, rather quietly and clearly, "This job is killing you." That's all it needed to say, and all I needed to hear. In my mind, I was outta there. None of my family or friends were the slightest bit surprised when I told them about my plans to resign. All of them had understood, when I left for France, that I would soon part company with Peat, and with that kind of pace. I still wonder why I was the last to know.

Upon my departure from that job, I gleefully gave myself a year off to continue the journey that had begun to unfold in France, to let my mind and heart continue to unfold. For that year, whenever I napped during an afternoon, I felt ancient fatigue sloughing off. One year merged into the next, the money held out, and at exactly the end of the second year, two major events happened, within one week of each other. First, a major consulting client found me (someone I'd known five years earlier), and I began a thirty-month run with his organization. And then I met the woman who would become my major wife. She and I are well past the thirty-month point, and we plan a much, much longer run. And the rest (in more than one sense of that term) was history.

The life I lead today doesn't resemble how I lived in 1997. This kind of transformation can happen when we step outside our assumptions and our routines, and venture into the unknown. In fact, just about anything can happen. Perhaps that's why we don't do grinding halts very often. It's hard to get full-hearted support from ourselves, from our beloveds, and from others who count on us to be and remain as we are. Taking such leaves of our senses would threaten to upset too many applecarts.

That's my story and, as a friend once put it, it's sticking to me. Here's what I make of the journey that I've portrayed in my story:

- It's never too late to come home to yourself. And such home-coming is necessary if you wish to do more than simply hang around the planet, as I had been doing; and

- There are many practices—many bells of awakening, many still-points and stopovers—available to each of us, to keep us coming home to ourselves and to see to it that we never get too far afield in the first place. And so that we may never need to pull that emergency brake and grind to a halt. David Kundz's book talks about many such practices, and we can all learn something from his ideas. However, we all have our own innate wisdom, as well as our own storehouses of experience, to tell us what we need in order to become aligned with our lives, and to stay that way.

In closing, here's a little more from the Wordsworth sonnet: "The world is too much with us; late and soon/Getting and spending, we lay waste our powers/Little we see in Nature that is ours/We have given our hearts away."

I trust that this chapter has given you your words' worth.

Practice

1. Give yourself frequent stillpoints this week. Take one whenever you need a brief respite. Think about practices you can use for stillpoints of one minute or less, between meetings or tasks on your to-do list.

   - Adopt practices mentioned in this chapter, or utilize those that have been effective for you.

- When you feel the need for a stillpoint, take one. Fight the tendency to postpone it. Remind yourself that there will never be a better time than right now.

2. Plan a stopover for yourself: perhaps a half day, or even one or two full days, devoted to doing nothing special. Put the date in your calendar for sometime within the next month—earlier if you can. Enjoy planning what you will do (and what you won't do) during your stopover. Savor the buildup to it.

   Make sure to do whatever you need to do to protect the stopover time from being encroached on. Then, when stopover time comes, enjoy it to the hilt. The first task when you return from your Stopover: plan your next one.

3. Plan a stopover involving a special other person (spouse, partner, or friend) or your family. Propose the idea to others and engage them in the planning. Have fun with it.

4. If the idea of a grinding halt resonates with you, start planning yours now. Most likely, you'll need a few months to clear the calendar and clear off your desk. The sooner you begin the planning process, the sooner you can smoothly glide into that long stopover.

Chapter 26:
Joseph and the Amazing
Technicolor Mom

$\mathcal{M}$y wife is a smart, healthy woman. ("Healthy," she often reminds me, "is not the same as normal." Point well taken.)

I'm reminded of that fact quite vividly today. This evening will be opening night for West High's production of *Joseph and the Amazing Technicolor Dreamcoat*, and my stepson—Jody's son, Aman—is none other than Joseph. Last night was the dress rehearsal, and the three of us were there: Jody, me, and the Panasonic camcorder that she had just purchased. Only two of us truly saw the production (which, by the way, was nothing short of spectacular; a little ragged, as you might expect from a dress rehearsal, but also gorgeous, rollicking, tuneful, and more than a little over the top). Last night, I saw the musical. The Panasonic recorded the musical. And Jody saw the LCD screen.

Peering through that two-and-one-half-inch screen, she couldn't take in the full magnitude of what the rest of us experienced. When Aman appeared, all six feet one inches of him (six-seven if you count his Afro), in his truly amazing technicolor creamcoat, she couldn't fully see this luminescent, glistening figure light up the stage and, for all I know, the entire ZIP code. Also, she didn't get to see my eyes widen and my jaw drop. She didn't see Joseph's brothers and their wives—these amazing young men and women literally bursting with talent and performing with abandon—rollick and frolic and hit their marks. No, she saw it all through the tiny screen, and she's well aware of what she missed.

So tonight the camera stays home. Just the two of us will attend opening night. It's the musical's opening night, and in a way, it's opening night for Jody's eyes too. She'll watch the stage, and I'll watch her face. I want to see her eyes widen (and perhaps moisten) and her jaw drop. She deserves it. As I often tell her, "Honey, you've been like a mother to that boy." And during this past week of final rehearsals, she's truly stepped into the mom role big-time, doing everything necessary to keep Aman healthy and nourished, limit his sleep deprivation (show me a teenager, and I'll show you someone sleep deprived), and generally clear his path to show time. She's well aware of what she's let go of this week: some progress on her dissertation, some of her own sleep, and the belief that she was in command of her time. She made a conscious, healthy decision to mobilize in just this way, just for this week. Because she's a mom, because she's smart, and because she's healthy.

Here's the back-story: Jody is agonizingly aware that Aman will graduate West High School in June. Most likely, he'll go away to college somewhere, and her life will change dramatically. Yes, her time will become more nearly her own. But she would eagerly trade some of that Jody time for more contact with her only, and much-treasured, child. She became clear on her priorities several months ago in contemplating her doctoral studies, her newly formed consulting business, and Aman's looming graduation. She needed to maximize her being truly available for Aman in this capstone period of his emerging young adulthood. She resolved not to miss a moment of it, while still going full out on the dissertation and assembling the foothills of a consulting practice.

Business travel and shameless self-promotion will be minimized in the short run, and both will undoubtedly accelerate as this period draws to a close. She's sacrificed some savings to get a good video camera, and sacrificed actually seeing the dress rehearsal in order to get it on tape. She knows that, with the recording safely behind her, tonight is her time to feast. And tomorrow night as well. And then she'll speak of it relentlessly, until next Friday and Saturday nights. We'll attend all four performances. She doesn't want to miss a moment of it … and I don't want to miss a moment of her taking it all in. Because I'm also smart, and I'm also healthy. And healthy, to be sure, is not the same as normal.

Postscript: Opening Night was everything we could have asked for. The cast and the audience were full of adrenalin, and we all played our roles perfectly. From the torrent of applause that greeted Erin, the young woman who welcomed the audience to opening night, clear through to the standing ovation that accompanied Aman's final bow, it was a real celebration. And Jody, in case you were wondering, took it all in and kvelled (that's Yiddish for, well … for *kvelled*) the whole time. At intermission, she made a beeline for the hallway, for two Mom Reasons. One was to buy the one remaining blue Joseph T-shirt (it has Aman's likeness on it) in his size. And the other was to have her fifteen minutes of fame as a celebrity mom. With so many neighbors, soccer parents, band parents, and cast parents milling around, she went for a victory lap. And I say, why not? She's been like a mother to that boy.

Post-postscript: Yesterday, about eight months after our week of Joseph, I mentioned to Jody that I finally got it about Aman's role. I explained that while playing our Joseph DVD for friends the previous evening, and hearing the narrator sing "Jacob and Sons," I suddenly realized that Aman as Joseph was playing the role of *Jacob's son* … basically, Jody's and my last name. I had known when we got married that Jody had gleefully changed her last name as a kind of homecoming. Had she been born a boy (which would have entirely screwed up my plans, of course), her parents would have named her Jacob. So in marrying me, she was getting the best of both worlds: she was getting the name Jody Jacobson, which she finds melodious, and she was finally getting the name Jacob that she would have had, if she had been born a boy. Her response to my brilliant epiphany was pure puzzlement. "I don't understand it. You were with me during intermission of each of the performances, and you heard me explain to people, time and again, that Aman's playing Joseph had special meaning for me: the whole Jacob's son thing." Oh well …

Practice

Many of us, myself included, love to capture Kodak moments to savor in the future—so much so that we sometimes come away with a photographic (or video or audio) record, but with amnesia for the event itself.

If this describes you, be sure to strike a balance between the following two savoring practices. Each requires somewhat different energy and focus:

- **Absorption:** really being immersed in the event itself, savoring it in real time

- **Kodak Moments:** taking photos, buying souvenirs, collecting drink coasters, and the like

In planning your next vacation trip or other big event, ask your companion(s) to help you maintain a healthy balance between being present while you're there (being absorbed) and being behind the camera (capturing a Kodak moment). And when you're there, practice really being there.

Chapter 27:
Deeply Grounded Listening

*T*he phrase *deeply grounded listening* popped into my head as I sat down to write. It refers to an important facet of communications that I hadn't thought about in those terms. I'd initially intended to write about three appreciative questions (variations on a theme), but as I thought about these questions, I realized that they share the theme that's summarized by this chapter's title: deeply grounded listening. So, I'd like to explore this form of listening and what it might mean. In the next chapter, I'll tackle the three appreciative questions in context of this kind of listening. And I'll write about the appreciative act of listening, and about asking nothing at all; just listening.

Can you remember having a conversation with someone in which they were so present that you felt free (and you felt invited) to explore anything you wanted to, to go as deep as you desired, to follow whatever weird tangents might arise, and simply to say whatever wanted saying? If so, then you were in the presence of someone who was practicing deeply grounded listening. The person's mental state and demeanor probably pulled you in. He established a container that welcomed you and held you safely and securely, so you could explore freely and go where you needed to go.

The most recent time I can remember such an experience was just before the Christmas holidays, when my wife suggested that we speak with each other about how our respective work was going, our vision for that work, what's fascinating us in it these days, what lines of thought we're pursuing, what we're excited about. We each took turns, and the only ground rule was that the listener would just listen. The only questioning the person could do was for purpose of clarification. (The "just listen" part was her idea. The clarification part was mine. I probably didn't think I was truly capable of just listening.)

When it was my turn to speak, I felt a freedom to explore, to pursue lines of thinking that were new (and that were news) to me, to hear myself think aloud. I felt relieved and expansive at the sense of safety I felt in exploring, exhilarated to hear myself riff in unanticipated directions, and surprised and delighted at where my thinking (and Jody's listening) took me. I felt grateful for the opportunity to speak from my mind and heart about my work. Thinking back upon it now, I also recall being delighted at how daring I dared to be, in dreaming big about my work, more than I typically let myself do in my everyday mind. And, because of Jody's patient listening and her feedback at the end, I felt celebrated.

If I were appreciatively interviewing you about a time when you were listened to in a deeply grounded way, I would invite you to tell me the story of that time, with all the details you'd care to supply. I'd ask you how you felt, being listened to in such a deep and present way. And I'd ask about what happened as a result: to the conversation, to you, and to the relationship. Come to think of it, if I were really cooking, I'd be practicing the very kind of deep listening that I was inquiring about.

I think of deeply grounded listening as involving five core qualities. First, the listener is there for you. Second, there's safety. Third, there's a connection between speaker and listener. And fourth, there's compassion flowing from listener to speaker. And finally, there is spaciousness. Let's explore each of them.

The Listener is There for You. The conversation, or at least the portion of it that's devoted to your airtime, is about you. It's not about the listener. It's not even about what a good (or deeply grounded) listener the person is. It's about the listener's establishing the container for you to explore and go wherever your mind and heart need to take the conversation. The listener has put aside her ego needs. Not easy to do, but a vital component.

Safety. In the situation, it's okay, and it's safe, for you to touch on whatever topic, to go however deep, wide, or weird, and to use whatever voice is needed to serve you. Safety seems to mean the listener is without agenda, without judgment, and, again, without ego. (The speaker, of course, is free to inject as much ego as he likes. After all, this is about him.)

Connectedness and Compassion. The listener communicates—less through words and more with nonverbal grunts, facial behavior, posture, nods, and the like—that he is with you, that he feels connected to you and to what you're saying. He skillfully conveys this connectedness with commendable economy. The listener's communication facilitates the flow; it doesn't interrupt it. Inherent in this feeling of being connected is that he senses your experience, and experiences it as though he were in your shoes, which, of course, isn't possible. So it's an approximation, but a vivid one, that allows the person to feel compassion (literally, with feeling) for you and for your experience. Deeply grounded listeners find a way to convey that compassion without intruding. Typically, that means that less is more on the listener's part. Again, this is not particularly easy to do, but it's a vital part of this kind of intimate listening, and each of us can learn how to do it.

Spaciousness. A final core quality is that the listener is spacious. This is a hard quality to describe, but we know it when we feel spacious in our own listening, and when we're speaking with someone who's listening spaciously to us. When disclosing ourselves to such a listener, we sense that she feels equally interested and available—no matter the topic we choose, and no matter the direction in which we take that topic. To this person, it's all good, as are we.

That doesn't mean she is neutral about us, what we're saying, or about her hopes and aspirations for us. Far from it. But somehow, spacious listening allows us to navigate anywhere we need to go, and to finally land at home. T. S. Eliot expresses it beautifully in *The Wasteland*: "And the end of all our exploring will be to arrive where we started and know the place for the first time."

For me, it's a real privilege to be listened to and to be heard from such a deeply grounded place. One measure of the quality of our lives may be the number of occasions in which we're on either end of this kind of communication—and whether the ratio is close to one to one. Here's what I mean:

- If you're doing more deeply grounded listening than being listened to in that manner, you may need to ask your listener for more airtime, or to be listened to in a different way. Or you may need to find a different conversational partner for this purpose. Not everyone can be there for us in this way. But someone, *many* someones, can.

- Conversely, if you're the recipient of deeply grounded listening more than often than you are the giver, you may need to practice such listening a little more. I have faith that doing so will enrich the other person, and that it will bring you to a deeper and richer appreciation of the times when you are the recipient. I'm sure of it.

Here are five questions to help you reflect on your experience of listening in a deeply grounded way:

• What's your ratio?

• How frequently do you practice being a deeply grounded listener?

• What helps you to show up in that way?

• How does the conversation change when you listen in a deeply grounded way?

• When you find that you're not listening that way, how do you recoup and listen more deeply?

In the coming week, take deeply grounded listening to heart in your own listening to clients, colleagues, family, and of course, to yourself. See what happens.

Practice

1. Recall a time when you were listened to in a deeply grounded way about something that was important to you. (It may help to close your eyes during this practice, and envision the situation as a play in which you are playing yourself.) As you relive this experience, pay attention to these aspects of the experience:

    • What are you speaking about?

    • How are you speaking about it?

    • What is the person doing? (Think about his posture, eye contact, tone of voice, and so on.)

    • What is the person saying?

- How do you know the person is listening in a deeply grounded way?
- What effect is his mode of listening having on you?

In reflecting on this scene,

- What do you learn about deeply grounded listening, and its power?
- What insights do you glean for your own ability to practice this form of listening?

2. Recall a time when you listened in a deeply grounded way to someone who was relating something that was important to him. (Again, it may help to close your eyes during this practice, and envision the situation as a play in which you are playing yourself.) As you relive this experience, pay attention to these aspects of the experience:

- What is the other person speaking about?
- How is he speaking about it?
- What are you doing? (Your posture, eye contact, tone of voice, and so on.)
- What are you saying?
- How do you know you're listening in a deeply grounded way?
- What effect is this mode of listening having on the other person? On you?

In reflecting on this scene,

- What do you learn about your ability to listen in a deeply grounded way, and the effect such listening has on the other person, and on you?

- What insights do you glean for how you can practice this form of listening more frequently?

3. Consider each of the following five core qualities of deeply grounded listening:

- Being there for the person
- Creating a safe climate for exploration
- Forging a sense of connection between speaker and listener
- Feeling compassion for the person and his situation
- Being spacious

    Then answer these two questions:

- When you are at your best as a listener, how do you demonstrate this specific quality, e.g., what are you doing when you're truly there for someone?

- What can you do to practice this skill more of the time?

Chapter 28:
Deeply Grounded Questions,
And Just Listening

*I*n chapter 27, I foreshadowed that I would use this chapter to introduce three appreciative questions, each one designed to take our conversations in deep and important directions. All three are variations on a deceptively simple and profound question: "Is there anything you would like to add?" I'll introduce the questions in the order in which I encountered them. See if any of them resonate with you. Then I'll ponder whether we could be better listeners by just listening.

The first question couldn't be simpler or more elegant: "Anything else?" George Kinder used that question in demonstrating empathic listening during his two-day Seven Stages of Money Maturity™ workshop, which I took in July 1999. Subsequently, he and Susan Galvan made "Anything else?" the touchstone question in the Kinder Institute for Life Planning's training for financial life planners. I have come to know this question well, in experiencing that training and subsequently becoming a trainer and mentor in the Institute. We train planners to listen spaciously to responses to questions such as "Why are you here today?" and "What would you like to be saying about our work together, in twelve months?" By repeating "Anything else?" until the client indicates "No, that's all," what transpires is akin to peeling an onion: more and more is revealed. In asking this question, less is more. Nothing needs to be added. And when asked with heartfelt intentionality, it never sounds contrived. I've increased my use of "Anything else?" lately, and I am always struck by its economy and its power. Thank you, George.

The second question—"Is there anything else you would like to tell me?"—is used by Rachel Naomi Remen, MD, when she teaches medical students and residents. By learning to ask that question calmly, while being fully attentive to the patient, and without reaching for the door or the prescription pad, the physician allows the patient to explore and reveal signs, symptoms, hopes, despair, and anything else that's in there. Her book, *Kitchen Table Wisdom*, is a compassionate and moving account of what it means to be a physician, a patient, a person. So, too, is its sequel, *My Grandfather's Blessings*.

The third question, and the one I've encountered most recently, is rather similar to Dr. Remen's question, "Is there anything else you would like to tell me?" However, it has a subtle difference that worked beautifully when I heard it. The question is, "Is there anything that I haven't asked you ... that you would like to say?" Jody, my part-time consulting partner and full-time wife, recently asked this question of her client after they had fully discussed several major aims of the project on which Jody subsequently delivered breakthrough results. The answer to that question came swiftly, pointing her in a direction that planted itself firmly in her mind, and which served as a beacon for the ensuing work. My wife treasures clarity, and she asks, "Is there anything that I haven't asked you ... that you would like to say?"—among other questions—to help clients and herself gain clarity.

Each of these three great questions is commendably simple and brief. Each only works its magic, however, if the listener can convey that (a) she really wants to know the answer, and (b) she doesn't have anywhere else to be.

In the previous chapter, I mentioned that with deeply grounded listening, less is more. After writing that chapter, I revisited *Kitchen Table Wisdom* and opened the book at random to a brief chapter called "Just Listen." Dr. Remen's words are eloquent and powerful. I invite you just to listen.

> Perhaps the most important thing we ever give each other is our attention ... [T]here's no need to do anything but receive them ... Listen to what they're saying. Care about it. Most times caring about it is even more important than understanding it ... It has taken me a long time to believe in the power of simply saying, "I'm so sorry," when someone is in pain. And meaning it.

Dr. Rumen cautions us to let the person tell her story without interruption, without sharing your own story, and without trying to produce a wise response. She then gives us a profound maxim about just listening. "A loving silence often has far more power to heal and to connect than the most well intentioned words."

Whenever I read her writing, I feel a calm spaciousness come over me. At the same time, I am seized with the mad desire to rush out and find someone who wants to talk, and listen the heck out of them—to just listen. The quoted passage has deeply grounded me so that I can more effectively carry out the sacred job of listening.

Practice

1. Reflect on these questions:

- How comfortable are you just listening? What happens, within you and in the situation, when you just listen? Conversely, what happens when you don't?

- Who do you know who is good at just listening? What happens when the person has listened to you in that way? What lessons can you draw from this, for your own listening practice?

2. This week, practice just listening without the intention to (a) fix the person or the situation, (b) make the person feel better, or (c) dispel your own discomfort with what is being said. Observe what happens.

3. Consider the three questions introduced in this chapter:

- Anything else?
- Is there anything else you would like to tell me?
- Is there anything I haven't asked you ... that you would like to say?

This week, be alert to opportunities to experiment with asking one or more of these questions, or any variations that seem fitting. See where it leads.

Chapter 29:
Replenishing the Doll-Maker's Supplies

*L*ike many of you, I'm self-employed. Actually, that's an illusion. It's probably truer to say that I'm rented by the following: coaching clients, organizations I consult with, strategic partners with whom I have delightful roles, readers and listeners whom I may never meet, associations and other organizations for whom I make presentations and deliver workshops, and the like. It's no wonder I sometimes feel so scattered. I have so many bosses!

Where was I? Oh, self-employed. One of the joys of this self-employment is that I get to have many offices: the condo I use as my office of record, my home, the neighborhood Caribou Coffee, the Ashman Branch of the Madison Public Library, the local Borders Books and Music, and a few others. I can place my body in any one of these spaces that calls out to me, depending on my purpose and mood. They're all my favorites. When I sense that I'm in need of replenishing my storehouse of ideas, I head for Borders for a couple of hours. I prefer going on weekdays, when it's inhabited by a manageable number of infants and their moms, retirees, a few students, and for all I know, a couple of people who suffer as I do from delusions of self-employment.

Here's my Borders ritual: I get my tea or coffee, stake out a table, and then browse through the new nonfiction tables and shelves containing business, psychology, self-help, and books on any other topic that beckons me. I scoop up five or six books that attract my eye, and I return to my table, amply equipped for the next hour or two. I never start at the beginning of a book. I open, seemingly at random, to various pages of various volumes. Invariably I encounter a cornucopia of delights, as well as new topics to write about. And yes, I occasionally buy one or two of the books, as I did this morning. I'm not (entirely) a freeloader, and I know that Borders' shareholders are counting on me. I view the price of the books as rent on the space and furniture.

I thought it might be fun to present a few quotes from one of this recent morning's books, and add my own free associations to each. The book is boldly titled *Ballsy: 99 Ways to Grow a Bigger Pair and Score Extreme Business Success*, by Karen Salmansohn. Here goes:

"Know thy limitations. Whenever possible, delegate what you suck at." The author's recommendation is exactly what I urge my coaching and consulting clients to do, although I typically don't phrase it that way. I often give them a simple criterion as to how to select and prioritize from among their many choices of activities. I tell them to assess where their greatest ROY is. (No, not ROI, or return on investment.) ROY stands for *return on you*. They always seem to intuitively grasp that it refers to what they can uniquely do by virtue of their skills, passions, and position. So many of them know that they are spending large amounts of time on activities that don't provide substantial returns (however computed), but in which they feel trapped. The ROY concept seems to serve as a bell of awakening for them.

"Use your mornings to get fired up, and aim yourself like a human cannonball at your goals!" I just love the vivid image of a human cannonball, and its inherent contradiction with how my body feels on most mornings. Actually, I've begun to think of it in terms of hurtling myself toward my destiny. The point is that the only moment I can do something about is the present one. That's where I'm accountable to myself. Salmansohn's advice and the cannonball metaphor remind me that I can aim myself in any direction in each moment. I have a choice. I've begun to focus on what it's like to feel choiceful, and what leads a person to feel that way. A lot of my coaching work has taken on that focus.

"When faced with a problem, substitute someone you trust and respect as being in your place—and imagine what they would do." This is almost identical to what I touched on in chapter 7: "What Would Your Favorite Hero Do?" I have become familiar with this practice in the last few years and have used it occasionally with myself. Sometimes I substitute the Buddha; sometimes my wife, Jody; sometimes my late friend and mentor, Ruth. They're all wise people, and they never fail me. It's an amazingly apprecative question, in that it taps into our visions of our wisest, most effective role models that we can muster for a given circumstance. As I have grown to have a stronger sense of who I am, what I stand for, and what I won't stand for, I've modified the question: I now ask myself, "What would I do here, if I were truly present and on top of my game?" It's funny how quickly the right action springs into mind. I believe that people possess great wisdom, and that my job is to help them access that wisdom. Apparently, by asking myself, "What would I do here, if I were truly present and on top of my game?" I tap into my own inner gyroscope. Try it for yourself, and see if it works for you.

A note about the Salmansohn book: I was both intrigued and repulsed by its title. We don't talk that way around here. It's simply not the Wisconsin way. However, I was quickly won over by its medium *and* its message; the contents are not only true to its title, but surprisingly insightful and wise. And the book is gorgeously and creatively designed, with pizzazz and energy. If you thumb through it, I think you'll be delighted by its zany creativity, and you'll agree with my impression that it was designed by a deranged individual. A postscript: as I was reading through it I realized I already own a book by the same author. You might love its title, as I do: *How to Be Happy, Dammit: A Cynic's Guide to Spiritual Happiness.*

You might be wondering about this chapter's title, "Replenishing the Doll-Maker's Supplies." Anne Lamott, a wonderful writer about the craft of writing, believes there's no such thing as writer's block. She thinks it's actually writer's emptiness. In *Bird by Bird*, she likens the writer to a doll-maker living in the attic. When her production of rag dolls dries up, it's not because she's blocked. She's simply run out of rags. You don't need to send her to a therapist, have her go on retreat, or dispatch her to a doll-maker's camp. All you need to do is gather a new supply of rags, climb on a ladder, and hand them up to her. Then wait for her to her convert them to riches. For me, that's what going to Borders is about. I do it for the rags.

Practice

"Know thy limits. Whenever possible, delegate what you suck at."

1. Identify two or more things that you "suck at." For each one, answer these questions:

    *   Does this task need to be done at all? If not, cross it off your to-do list.

    *   If it must be done, can you trade with someone who will do it (e.g., can you do something he sucks at)?

    *   If you must perform the task, can you increase your efficiency and effectiveness at it?

- Can you change your attitude toward it?

2.   Here's a practice that can powerfully reinforce your doing something you don't have a choice about doing—including things you suck at:

- List a few things you have zest and zeal about doing.

- Do one thing that you suck at for fifteen minutes, and reward yourself by immediately doing fifteen or thirty minutes of one of the zestful activities.

    Over time, the opportunity to perform the zestful activity only after doing the one you suck at will reinforce your doing what you have to do first. (Eat your vegetables if you want dessert. Same principle.)

"Use your mornings to get fired up, and aim yourself like a human cannonball at your goals!"

3.   The following practice is taken from Jackie Kelm's study, as reported in chapter 12:

- Upon arising, create an intention for the day. Specifically, answer the question, "What is one thing, large or small, that I could do today to increase my joy?" If the prospect of joy doesn't fire you up, substitute a different feeling state. For example, happiness, contentment, peacefulness, excitement, and so on. Find a feeling that you think will fire you up. See what happens.

"When faced with a problem, substitute someone you trust and respect as being in your place—and imagine what he would do."

4.   Check out the practices in chapter 7 on this topic.

Chapter 30:
Lifting People out of
Their Everyday Minds

$\mathcal{H}$ ave you ever heard someone say something, and suddenly everything came together for you? The person may not have intended to address what's on your mind, what's cooking below your mind's surface, or what you need most at that time. It could even be a phrase on a billboard that catches your eye as you speed toward the airport. Whatever form it takes, it's a truly amazing moment when it happens. It's akin to the experience when a massage therapist works on a muscle until it relaxes and slips into place, and your body suddenly feels coherent again: *Ahhhh*.

It's not just that the experience feels good. It's that something important has been revealed, something that allows you to integrate disparate things that have been trying to come together, but for which you've lacked the key to unlock their unity—that is, until that very moment. I know this is so because it happened to me recently. Here's the story.

A couple of months ago, I was attending a presentation by George Kinder, during the annual conference of the Kinder Institute of Life Planning. George was interviewing Marty Valente, a friend from California, to demonstrate the process of lighting the torch (*Lighting the Torch* is also the title of George's book, coauthored by Susan Galvan, the institute's cofounder). In the course of describing his own work, Marty said, "What I'm really trying to do is to lift people out of their everyday minds."

For me, the notion of lifting people out of their everyday minds was a true bell of awakening. I said to myself, "Of course! That's what we're all trying to do—those of us who try to bring others (and ourselves) to a greater wholeness, joy, fulfillment, contribution, or whatever transformative purpose they are working toward." Then I thought, "That's what all spiritual traditions seek to do: to strengthen people's capacities to bring extraordinary mind or extraordinary heart to our ordinary, everyday situations."

Numerous practices seek to strengthen this ability. Some that come to mind include prayer, meditation, yoga, journaling, the taking of sacred vows, Bible reading, and belonging to a *sangha* (a community of like-minded practitioners). The same can be said of many forms of psychotherapy, counseling, and coaching. Appreciative Inquiry, as an approach and a philosophy, seeks to identify the ingredients of the extraordinary (our "highest and best moments") and use them planfully, skillfully, and frequently, to enhance of the lives of people, organizations, and communities.

The phrase "lifting people out of their everyday minds" has continued to resonate in my mind. It functions as a beacon for me: a vivid image that beautifully illustrates what I'm after. Perhaps I chose my work in order to more deeply develop my ability to lift myself out of my everyday mind, to do my life better, in more graceful, vigorous, influential, loving, and useful ways. Of course, I know that doing so will serve me. However, I also know that if I'm successful at it, anyone who's around me will also benefit. That's a big win-win. And looking through the other end of the telescope, if I offer practices that help others be their best selves, then they will benefit and I'll get better at my own practice. Again, everyone wins. It's what people mean when they say, "What goes around comes around."

You might be wondering, "What is this everyday mind, and where do we go when we're lifted out of it?" Whenever I think about my own everyday mind, I flash on thoughts such as: What's in it for me here? What will others think of me? How am I doing in this situation? How dare he talk to me that way? Am I being seen as bright (clever, compassionate, spontaneous, or whatever) in this situation? If they get *X*, there will be that much less of *X* available for me. If I don't get this contract (or this response, or this electronic gizmo), I'll really be upset!

What unites these manifestations of everyday mind is what George brilliantly calls "The linchpin of I, me, or mine." In his landmark book, *The Seven Stages of Money Maturity*, he describes the "structure of suffering" as a process whereby the individual causes himself distress by indulging in a variety of so-called innocent (half-true) thoughts that are inevitably accompanied by difficult feelings, and all of these are held together by internal storylines about I, me, or mine. George's prescription for breaking the grip of the structure of suffering is simple but profound: let the thoughts go, and let the feelings be. Simple, but not easy. It's a lifetime journey, which is why we call it a practice. I engage in it a lot. It's one of my touchstones. Sometimes I'm more skillful in applying it, sometimes less so.

And what happens when we lift ourselves out of that everyday state of mind? Whenever I do that, I experience greater feeling of spaciousness of my body, mind, and spirit; more generosity and spontaneity; a big increase in my perceived options in the situation; more creative solutions and innovative ideas; lots of gratitude ... and an unusually large amount of smiling. I wonder if any of those responses are true for you. And what you can add from your own experience.

Many chapters in this book present practices to help us lift ourselves out of our everyday minds. Here's one such practice from chapter 3: "Letting Our Souls Catch up with Us": the two-minute drill. I give myself ten minutes before beginning a coaching session. (In sports, the phrase "two-minute drill" is used with precision. I have applied it here with a large dose of poetic license.) I glance at my notes from the most recent session, get my physical space all set, and meditate for five to ten minutes, following my breath and visualizing my unwavering positive image of my client. This practice works wonders. I feel a connectedness, openness, and receptivity that I'm sure I wouldn't otherwise feel.

I've discovered, however, that there's such a thing as being too calm and centered. Last week, I executed my drill to perfection, or so I thought. There I was, calm and serene, with my water glass, paper, pen, and clock nearby—exquisitely centered and prepared. When the phone rang, I was startled to hear it … clear across the room! I laughed heartily at myself ("Mr. Mindfulness strikes again!") while scrambling for the phone. I picked it up, still laughing, and explained that the source of my amusement was none other than myself and my egotistical pride about how mindful I was being. This taught me a valuable lesson: laughing at my ego is another good way to lift myself above my everyday mind.

Weird Postscript Department

Late-breaking news! I sent Marty a completed draft of this chapter and asked his permission to identify him by name. He quickly e-mailed me this rather startling reply: "You're very kind to cite me in your article. The only thing is, those words 'lifting people out of their everyday minds' came from you when you were coaching on my elevator speech during the Kinder mentorship program. But if you want to cite me as you have, I am fine with that. They are great words."

Any recollection of specifics of that conversation has vanished from my memory banks. Here's what might have taken place: I may have summarized what I heard Marty saying, and then replied, "So what you're saying is that your work is about lifting people out of their everyday minds."

Go figure.

Practice

Here is a self-guided inquiry process about your own times of lifting yourself out of your everyday mind. Think back to an occasion when you were able to transcend the trap of I-me-mine, and avoid or dispel a structure of suffering. Then answer these questions:

- What was the situation?

- What were its challenges for you?

- How did you avoid or overcome the trap of I-me-mine?

- When everyday mind evaporated, what happened within you, and in the situation?

And here's the payoff question:

- What can you do to have more experiences of that sort?

Chapter 31:
An Abundant Thanksgiving Week

*M*y mind's been cooking lately about the rapidly approaching Thanksgiving holiday and the piece I've wanted to write about having an appreciative Thanksgiving Day. Then a new notion arose: why not think about an *abundant* Thanksgiving Day? I love the concept of abundance. It can refer to financial or material abundance, but it embraces much more than that. I conceive of it as a sense of fullness and ripeness, brimming with life in various sectors of our lives: financial, familial, spiritual, religious, community, work, health, psychological … The list of abundance areas goes on and on. In fact, I've created an instrument called the Life Abundance Portfolio©, which gives people the opportunity to explore their sense of abundance in a range of key areas in their lives. So, let's call it an abundant Thanksgiving Day and explore what that might consist of.

When I think of an abundant Thanksgiving, I think first of food. Then my mind goes to the people who have gathered together. Whether it's a small family dinner, a large group of friends and family, or a gigantic church dinner, there's generally good cheer and, at the very least, a temporary cease-fire. We tacitly agree to put aside our differences and our weapons of mass reactivity. We break bread together instead of bristling at Aunt Maud or grimly tolerating cousin Max. We enjoy the good fellowship while we can. Someone is likely to say that we should do this more often, and not just on our national Turkey Day.

Instead of simply nodding your agreement, respond instead with, "What a wonderful idea! How can we make that happen?" See what energies arise in both you and others. Maybe a couple of you who have enthusiasm for the idea can work together to make it happen. It only takes a couple of committed people. Recall Margaret Mead's classic statement: "Never doubt that a small group of thoughtful, committed citizens can change the world; indeed, it's the only thing that ever has."

Thinking more about an abundant Thanksgiving Day, I think about gratitude and thanksgiving, and then about the people who spend Thanksgiving Day either alone, in prison, or in the hospital. Then I call to mind people on a street in a far-off land or, with alarming frequency, in our cities and even our rural areas. It's a stretch for some of us (myself included) to hold the uncomfortable paradox of being surrounded by abundance while knowing that others near and far are so much less blessed materially. I wonder how other people make peace with that paradox, while at the same time asking someone to pass that fabulous-looking stuffing. This Thursday at Thanksgiving dinner with my family, I intend to verbally acknowledge our own bounty and others' lesser material abundance, and vow to do more to contribute to these unknown others' well-being.

How might we honor the spirit of giving thanks this year, in a way that does two things:

- Creates as much appreciation as we can stand

- Addresses the question, "How can we get more of this sense of appreciation, more days of the year?"

Here are a couple of rituals of appreciation and abundance for Thursday, and three for the week leading up to the big day:

Thanksgiving Day

1. The host, or other designated appreciator (DA for short), can tap a glass with a spoon, get everyone's attention, and propose the following: "Could we capture the spirit of Thanksgiving by going around the table (or the room), with each of us saying two or three things that you feel especially grateful or thankful for today?" And the DA models the process by going first, thereby making it safe for people to be personal (and even profound) in their declarations. When everyone who wishes to has taken a turn, it might be appropriate for the DA to add, "I wonder if anyone has any thoughts about what we could do to have that sense of gratitude or thankfulness, not just today but more of the time?" And just wait. See what thoughts and insights are offered. If none arises, the DA might offer her own thoughts and leave it at that. And then, of course, pass the stuffing.

2. Alternatively, the DA can suggest after dinner (if a football game isn't on TV, and if everyone isn't in the throes of a tryptophan-induced nap) that folks share stories about a time during the past year when they felt especially blessed, in whatever area of their lives. Depending on the size of the gathering, it may be best not to go around the room. It might feel more comfortable and lead to a deeper experience to gather in threes or fours and give each person a couple or three minutes to tell his story to the listeners, whose job is simply to listen. Afterward, the DA might say, "Wow! Here are some things I learned in listening," relate what he heard, and wait to see who else wants to share.

The Week Before

1. Right now, look within yourself and around you, and name all the things you're grateful for. Then, at dinner this evening or tomorrow, report on your experience, mentioning a few of the items on your gratitude list. Invite others to do the same. Make the point that a day of thanksgiving doesn't always have to fall on the fourth Thursday in November. You might be surprised at who reports, and at what they say.

2. Before Thursday, make an abundance list. Write down the following abundance areas, or make up your own:

Family	Health
Work	Friends
Community	Finances
Religion/spirituality	Stuff (an iPod, a car that works, comfortable shoes, toothpaste)

    In one or more of the above areas, list the things you feel abundant about. Place a check mark next to items that you can do something about having more of. You might then jot down specific actions to take. You may find, however, that simply making a check mark serves to plant it in your mind and prompt you to take action. As always, do whatever works for you.

3. Here's a final exercise to do in your mind's eye before Thanksgiving Thursday: Picture each person with whom you'll be spending Thanksgiving Day. Mentally make the rounds of the anticipated dinner table. For all the people, silently identify what you love most about them, their most admirable qualities, or memories of happy times spent with them. Experience

the positive feelings that go with these positive memories. Repeat these mental rounds each day before Thursday, and watch what happens. You may find that it increases your sense of anticipation (which we can call anticipatory savoring) and your enjoyment of Thanksgiving Day. And because of the positive energy you'll be exuding when Thursday rolls around, you'll be amplifying others' enjoyment of the day.

I wish you and yours a Thanksgiving week filled with abundance and appreciation. And 364 other days like that.

Practice

1. Apply the first designated appreciator ritual during your Thanksgiving dinner, no matter how many people are around the table. Alternatively, apply the second designated appreciator ritual after the meal. (You can do either or both practices, even if you're dining alone. It may sound a little weird, but I've done it, and it works.) Almost invariably, when it's over, someone will express his thanks for your suggesting the exercise. After acknowledging their appreciation, ask the others, "How did this work for the rest of you?"

2. Before Thursday, make your own abundance list. Invite others in your household to make their own lists. On Thursday, suggest that all the people share their lists.

3. Invite members of your household to experience the pre-Thanksgiving guided imagery exercise of picturing who will be seated around the Thanksgiving dinner table. Ask them to share their images. Wonderful things can happen.

- Noting similarities between people in what they anticipate can be extremely confirming and enriching, and it can also increase the savoring when Thursday comes.

- Discovering differences in what is anticipated can broaden everyone's sense of abundance and increase understanding of one another's frames of reference—always a good thing.

4. At least once per month, review your own abundance list. See what happens when you unlink it from a milestone event like Thanksgiving and make it part of your ongoing routine.

5. Invite your family to conduct a monthly review of everyone's abundance list. It can become a meaningful family ritual.

Chapter 32:
A Sane Pre-holiday Rush
And a Savory Holiday

December holidays (Christmas, Hanukkah, Kwanzaa, and others I may not be aware of) are special in many ways, much of which can be expressed as *more:*

- More gift-giving

- More celebrating

- More eating and drinking

- More after-Christmas shopping (giving new meaning to the phrase "Many happy returns of the day")

And some less savory aspects:

- More societal expectation that we should be merry and celebratory as the holidays approach. And that we should carry the holiday spirit throughout December.

- More hype and advertising. The message is, "If you love your family and our economy, you'll go out and do your (market) share. Get out there and shop 'til you drop!" It's hard to keep our priorities straight and to remember what the holidays are about at their core. My understanding is that they weren't originally intended to account for 40 percent of annual sales.

We have two challenges in this frenetic month: (a) Moving through the pre-holiday period with as much calm and enjoyment as possible, while not buckling under the pressures of work, holiday shopping, and our mixed feelings about the upcoming holidays. (b) Being in the holiday period in a present and life-affirming way, without drowning in *more*. Here are some appreciative ways to deal with each of these challenges.

Pre-holiday Self-care

1. Give yourself many stillpoints. I introduced the stillpoint concept of Dr. David Kundtz in chapter 15. A stillpoint is a brief respite—a few seconds, or as much as a fifteen-minute break—that allows you to breathe and come back to yourself. We probably need more stillpoints than usual this week. Here's a starter kit of stillpoint opportunities:

   • waiting on line at the post office

   • pumping gas

   • making out holiday cards

   • writing a report

   • caring for a parent or infant

   This week, each stillpoint is an investment in our sanity.

2. Cultivate positive images of the upcoming holidays. Picture yourself happily immersed in the settings you'll be in. Get into the scene in your mind's eye. Picture who'll be there and what they (and you) will be wearing, smell the smells and taste the

food and drink, laugh the laughs, enjoy the private conversations, feel the crunch of the snow beneath your shoes or skis. The more senses you can employ, the more effective the image will be in creating a state of positive anticipation.

When you feel rushed or stressed this week, call to mind one or more of the above scenes, savor it for a moment, and then resume your business, refreshed and replenished. The more often you can focus on positive anticipation, (a) the more pleasant the pre-holiday activities will be, in and of themselves, and (b) the more enjoyable the ensuing holidays will be. Each time you focus on the positive anticipatory image, you train your brain to enjoy the holidays when they eventually arrive. You're feeding your brain positive messages like "holidays = good feelings."

If you find yourself unable to summon up those positive images, maybe you could give yourself a "good (i.e., a life-affirming) talking-to" (see chapter 19 for more on this). Seek the counsel of someone you trust, and talk about the upcoming holidays and how to enjoy them. If your holiday plans hold the promise of more distress than you wish to experience, maybe you need to consider modifying them. Positive anticipation is not meant to be happy talk. In Appreciative Inquiry, there's something called the constructionist principle. It tells us that in every situation, there's more than one truth. It's usually wisest to choose the truth that's most life-affirming. That's not happy talk; that's simply wise choosing.

Savoring the Holidays

Savoring is defined as the awareness of pleasure, and the devoting of deliberate attention to that experience. Heaven knows there'll be plenty of opportunity to be aware of pleasurable indulgences next week: the opening of presents, the look on recipients' faces as they express (or feign) delight and surprise, the offering of truly savory food and drink, the way-too-many football games and endless reruns of *Miracle on 34th Street*, and all the rest.

The more you focus on savoring each separate aspect of what goes on during the holidays, the more you'll enjoy them and the less taxed you'll be. If you've ever gone to a wine tasting, you may recall being instructed on wine mindfulness: how to view, swirl, smell, sip, swallow, and experience the wine. As a result, you probably paid a lot more attention to your experience, you tasted the wine more deeply and fully than usual, and you drank more mindfully. And you probably consumed less than you might otherwise have.

Applying that example to our holidays, we would try to approach each situation—each present opened, each meal, each drink, each video viewing, and so on—with greater intention to savor. We would devote deliberate attention to the experience. Fred Bryant and Joe Veroff at University of Chicago have researched how best to do that, as I discussed in chapters 14 through 16. Here are some of their recommended practices:

- We'd practice **absorption**: We'd fully immerse ourselves in holiday activities. We might even limit our conversation, from time to time, to savor the moment. It may be awkward to be silent and still in the midst of a holiday gathering, but you can create frequent stillpoints where you remember to pay attention to the experience.

- We'd also **share the experience with others**: When we not only go through an experience with others, but we also comment on how cool, how meaningful, and/or how enjoyable it is while we're in the midst of it, we deepen our savoring.

- We'd **build memories**. This may consist of creating Kodak moments. It may also consist of taking small mementos of particularly meaningful holiday events: a program from Christmas Eve services, a coaster from a restaurant, a souvenir from the place you visited over the holidays (you know, stuff you'd never buy if you were in your right mind), and so on.

There's no magic to savoring the holidays. There's just (a) mindfulness, (b) a conscious willingness to focus on the good stuff, (c) an intention to catch ourselves when we're on overload or going negative, and (d) using that awareness as a cue to give ourselves frequent breaks from the action (a.k.a. stillpoints). And, of course, purchasing some goofy souvenirs.

It works for me. How about you? Think about your practices for keeping your sanity in the lead-up to the holidays, and maximizing your joy, delight, and meaningfulness during them. Resolve to call upon them in this frenetic time.

Practice

In addition to applying the practices discussed in this chapter, consider the following practices:

1. Think about your own best practices for staying present and centered in the midst of intense or chaotic situations. When are you at your best in such circumstances? Reflect on how you can apply those practices to the lead-up to the holidays.

2. Think about who your most effective role models have been for weathering the pre-holiday buildup and the holidays themselves. What are their secret recipes for remaining centered? How can you apply those recipes? When feeling as though you're succumbing to holiday or pre-holiday stress, pause and ask yourself what your favorite hero would do. See what you discover.

3. On a three-by-five-inch index card (or on your PDA or as a screen saver on your computer), note the following three practices for savoring the holidays. For each one, make a note about how you can apply it. (For example: "Building memories: Use my video camera to capture special occasions.")

    • Absorption
    • Sharing the experience with others
    • Building memories

When the holidays are getting to you (when they're just too much, or not enough), review the three practices and see if they provide any insights and cues you can use.

Chapter 33:
A Year-End Review

*W*hat better way to celebrate and elevate the year that's rapidly drawing to a close than by conducting an appreciative year-end review?

I first began facilitating this type of review with one client group about four years ago. Just last week, we conducted our fourth annual one. And last year, Jody and I spent a good portion of our holiday week doing an Appreciative Inquiry of our marriage. As a result, I've become a big fan of taking the time to savor the blessings of the year and openly acknowledging its attendant challenges, losses, and unbidden tragedies. We know that it wasn't all good, and we shouldn't pretend otherwise.

Here are some practices for conducting an appreciative year-end review in your workplace. But first, three suggestions:

- Don't wait until after New Year's. It's guaranteed that all interest and motivation for doing this review will be lost, and last year will be, as they say, "sooo last week."

- Set aside an hour. You probably won't need more time, and you might use less. Don't rush through it.

- Do not substitute this retrospective for your annual lunch or dinner with staff members. Your associates, like armies, travel on their stomachs. Unlike an army (or perhaps like one), they rely on their eggnog around this time of year. Same thing for your family. Don't deprive them of their traditional holiday dinner, or they'll turn on you. It won't be pretty.

Practice

Here are some suggested steps. Feel free to adapt, modify, or discard any or all of them, and to grow your own.

For Your Work Group

1. Bring Your Work Group Together: Have a flip chart or two available.

2. Construct a Time Line: Demark January–December along the bottom at the bottom of the flip chart page. Divide the page into three horizontal stripes, using dotted lines to mark them off. Label the top one "Community/World," the middle one with the company or group name, and the third one "Personal."

3. Identify Notable Events: Ask people to brainstorm notable events that have taken place this year (they need not be positive, just notable), in the following three categories. And please remember the cardinal rule of brainstorming: everyone's right.

    *   Community/World Events. Using 2007 as an example, you can expect entries such as continuing war in Iraq, lead-up to primary elections, Dow hitting fourteen thousand, and other world-shattering events. Expect some surprises. None of us, no matter how much we fancy ourselves as news junkies, can retain twelve months of stuff in our conscious minds.

- Notable Workplace Highlights. Again, these may not be all positive.

- Notable Personal Highlights. Again, not all positive.

  This three-part exercise usually takes fifteen to twenty minutes. It jogs everyone's recollections and provides a nice container for a year's worth of events and recollections. It sets the stage for the next exercise: storytelling.

4. Storytelling: If the group size is seven or less, have each person take a turn doing the exercise. If eight or more, consider dividing folks into storytelling pairs. Have them tell stories of the following two sorts:

- A high point of the year for you at work

- A high point of the year for you in your personal life

  If you have seven or fewer people present, go around the group, giving each person one minute to state a high point for work and one minute for a personal life high point. Be generous with those who ramble a little, but then don't be shy about encouraging them to wrap it up. Everyone knows who the filibusterers are. (Being a certified filibusterer, I know this to be true). And everyone wants them to cut it short.

  For eight or more, have people form pairs. Give each member of the pair two minutes (i.e., one minute per high point story), then have them switch roles. When they're done, reconvene as a group. Have each person briefly state the highlights of each high point event that his partner related. The person can ask his storytelling partner for an accuracy check on what he said. You might want to write the workplace high points, and possibly the personal ones, on a flip chart page.

5. Envision the Year Ahead: Use an appreciative scenario to project ahead for the coming year. For example, with my client group, I used the following invitation: What is one daring-but-doable wish you have for yourself in your personal life in the coming year? And what is one daring-but-doable wish you have for yourself in your work life in the coming year? You can divide a flip chart page down the middle. Label one column "Personal," the other "Work." Write down key words as people call out their responses to the "daring-but-doable" question.

6. Wrap Up: When everyone is done, simply ask, "How was this appreciative year-end review for you?" There will likely be plenty of comments. This is a graceful way to achieve closure.

For Families

Apply the storytelling aspect (step 4) of the foregoing practice. For family storytelling, you can suggest stories about two high point events: one about work or school, the other for personal life. Unlike the work group version, where time is at more of a premium, you can allow five minutes per high point, so people can share stories, rather than just mentioning their high points.

When all have shared their stories, go around the table or room and ask for a high point story about your family in this past year. See what pops into people's minds. Then conclude with a question about hopes and wishes for the coming year. Phrase it in language that fits your kids' frames of reference: for example, a cool thing that I hope happens in the new year, or an awesome thing I'm wishing for in the new year. This is not intended as a magic wand or genie-in-the-bottle kind of question. Therefore, instruct them that the hope or wish be something that could happen, if everything were to fall into place.

A note on high points or notable events that are not appreciative: It's entirely possible (in both the workplace and family setting) that people will mention setbacks, losses, and the like. Be sure to make it safe and okay for them to include these. You can then encourage them to reflect for a moment on this question: what lessons have you learned from this event that will help you in the coming year? This is a graceful and effective way of acknowledging the adversities they have brought up and the impact that these events have had on them, and gently moving the person to embrace what is life-giving in them, even in the aftermath of a truly terrible happening.

A final note: You may already have a family tradition of year-end retrospectives, appreciative or otherwise. Feel free to adapt any of the suggestions and practices in this chapter to your current traditions. The beauty of a year-end appreciative review is that it permits us to use the calendar as a reminder to pause, acknowledge, and celebrate what is truly important. Think of it as an oasis: a fertile place for travelers to replenish and renew before forging onward.

Chapter 34:
My Year of Living Appreciatively

What if we aspired to make the coming year an entirely appreciative one for ourselves? I ask myself, "What would an entire year of living appreciatively be like?" It's sometimes difficult for me to remain mindful while just walking up a full set of stairs. What kind of lunatic would aspire to be appreciative for a whole year? And then I wonder, "Hmm, let's see ... Just how would we pull off such a cosmic stunt?" The sheer audacity and boldness of the notion fascinated me so I sat down and, as the Brits say, I had myself a think about it. Here's what I came up with.

For starters, we'd want to create a big intention: a vivid phrase or a compelling visual image. A New Year's resolution to be appreciative wouldn't cut it because such resolutions have such sorry track records. I believe in the anticipatory principle more than in New Year's resolutions. That principle tells us that if we create a compelling mental image of our future, one which stirs our emotions and energizes us, we'll be much more successful in bringing those aspirations into being. The positive mental image serves as a kind of beacon, pulling us toward a desired future state of affairs.

We might select a phrase to create such a beacon for a whole appreciative year. Here's the one I chose for myself: My Year of Living Appreciatively. For me, it has an action phrase (Living Appreciatively) that has forward-moving energy, and it has enough reach (My Year of ...) so that it feels wonderfully ambitious. It's also concise, so I can keep it in mind and visualize it. And let's face it. If it doesn't work out, I'm off the hook as of next December 31. All upside potential, no downside.

You might start by constructing a beacon for your own appreciative year. Please make it ambitious, concise, and energetic. Choose something like Nurturing the Art of Appreciation, or Building My Appreciative Muscles. You might want to take a moment now and jot down one or two candidates that jump to mind, before reading further.

Equipped with our beacons, the next step is to get a handle on what we'd be on the lookout to be appreciative about. Here are three that immediately occur to me, regarding my own beacon, as I write this.

The Gifts and Blessings of Family and Friends: When I think of this category, I first think of my wife and stepson. And next, my brother, my nephew and nieces, and assorted cousins and their families. And many friends, flung far and wide. When I think of this mob—especially my wife and stepson—I immediately think of this question: what gifts and blessings does each one bring to the world? Quite a few gorgeous qualities jump to mind. Which leads this next question: what gifts and blessings does each of them bring to me? It turns out that my second list of gifts and blessings has most of the items on the first one (e.g., they're not saving the good stuff for other people; I get to have my share), and it contains some others in addition. The added gifts and blessings are more intimate and personal, having to do with nurturance, sustenance, loving challenges, endless opportunity for personal and spiritual growth, and a twenty-four/seven mirror of who I am. (The mirror's always there, whether I want to look at it or not.)

If I can answer these two questions in a deep way about a given person on my list of treasured people, I can create an unwavering positive image of who that person is at the core. (Here's a quick example: my stepson described himself as *thoughtful* during a recent performance of his class on multicultural awareness, in which each student shouted a one-word self-description. I was amazed that his self-image corresponded so closely to my image of him.) Creating and holding that life-affirming image will guide and sustain me in my interactions with others, will deepen our relationship, will bring out their best, and allow me to be at my best with them as well. And when I envision this gaggle of unwavering positive images, I realize that I have assembled a far-flung community of relationships that define, elevate, inspire, and sustain me. This priceless knowledge, plus my internal photo album of unwavering positive images I hold of them, gives me a running start at My Year of Living Appreciatively.

The Magnificent Improbability of Life: This is no small topic. Actually, I'm a little stunned that I've dared to think it, much less to type it out and contemplate including it here. However, I feel called to do so. Having thought it and typed it, I'm finding that the phrase "the magnificent improbability of life" is now playing nonstop in my mind. Actually, it's doing more than playing. It's shouting, and it's demanding to be heard. In truth, I can't possibly grasp the infinitesimal likelihood of life being created anywhere in the universe—not to mention on our planet, in our solar system, in our very galaxy. And certainly not taking the form of this assemblage of body-mind-spirit-soul commonly known as Ed.

Think about it for a minute: how many different forces and entities needed to come together to create you in the first place! Not to mention the exquisitely complex and delicate environment needed to sustain you in this present moment, and in the next moment, and so on, for as many moments as you will be alive. It's huge. In fact, it must be what teenagers mean when they say, "That's awesome, man!"

So the phrase The Magnificent Improbability of Life is the second element contributing to My Year of Living Appreciatively. If I can summon it at least occasionally in the coming year, it will serve as a lens through which I can view beauty and kindness, and even behold cruelty and conflict. It will stop me in my tracks, encourage me to put down my weapons of mass reactivity, and be more spacious and compassionate in my encounters with others, not to mention with myself. And I will want to defuse or transform what is violent and destructive in the world, to allow more loving and life-giving actions to arise ... that is, when I can manage to summon that magnificent phrase about life's magnificent improbability. And I'm likely to take my own woes and my internal storylines less seriously. That alone would be worth the price of admission.

The Kindness of Strangers: While I was writing in a coffee shop today, the early morning sun was hitting me in the eyes. As I went over to lower the shade, the fellow sitting near the window said (in true Wisconsin style), "I see you've got the worst seat, in terms of the sun. How can I help?" He proceeded to lower the shade for me, which took care of the glare. I thanked him for his thoughtfulness. After a while, he left the place, and the sun continued to rise (as it usually does). It glared through an adjacent window, once again rendering me snow blind. The guy's replacement did the same thing as his predecessor. He saw me shielding my eyes with one hand as I attempted to write with the other, and he did a neat pantomime to indicate that he'd lower that shade, which again did the trick. We smiled and nodded to each other in a mutual ritual of bowing. So, thanks to these two Good Samaritans, I'm going to keep in mind the kindness of strangers, to help me to have My Year of Living Appreciatively. And I'm sure that keeping the kindness of strangers in mind will help me to be a kinder stranger. Will Rogers said, "A stranger is just a friend I haven't met yet."

Still more categories for practicing appreciation have occurred to me in the course of writing this. However, I've been schooled in the virtues of brevity, and I will practice it here. I'll leave the matter until sometime next year, in favor of wishing you a joyous New Year's celebration, and a great and joyous journey in your own year of living appreciatively.

Practice

Create a beacon for yourself for the coming year. My beacon is My Year of Living Appreciatively. If that one doesn't resonate for you, try substituting a different adjective, such as lovingly, healthfully, productively, mindfully, and so on. For example, your beacon might be Showing Love Above All Else, or Living a Productive Year. Create one that serves as a compelling, energizing, and motivating beacon for you. Then do the following four steps:

1. Imagine what living your beacon would be like. In this imagined year, what are you doing more of? Doing less of? Doing differently?

2. Equipped with your beacon, identify three or four areas or situations in which you will strive to apply that beacon. (Mine included family, strangers, and appreciating life for its very improbability.)

3. Think of specific situations in the coming year in which it would be a stretch for you to apply your beacon. Create an intention to show up in that way (appreciatively, lovingly,

mindfully, or whatever's in your beacon) in those circumstances.

4. Schedule a monthly review of your beacon. See how this periodic review serves to keep you on track toward your Year of Living Appreciatively.

Afterword: Now What?

I hope you have enjoyed and benefited from reading *Appreciative Moments*. I also hope you feel inspired and motivated by your experience with practices throughout the book, to continue on your journey of appreciation. Where do you go from here, fortified by what you have read and practiced? Here are four suggestions:

1. Keep the book handy, on your desk or nightstand, or otherwise within arm's reach. In your spare moments, do one or more of the following:

   - Skim the contents page. Read a chapter whose title entices you.

   - Browse through the book, looking at passages you may have underlined and notes you may have made in the margins.

   - Open at random and read a passage. (Some people believe there are no accidents. They would say that by letting your fingers do the walking, you will be guided to something that has meaning for you.)

2. Use the book as the basis of ongoing discussion among a group of friends. The peer support and reinforcement that groups provide can be important factors in strengthening our appreciative habits. Here are some options:

   - Form a study group to discuss the chapters and to experiment with the practices. A good size for such groups is five to eight members. Typically, such groups are called support groups or accountability groups. Given the subject matter, why not call yours an appreciation group?

- Book discussion groups are increasingly popular in this country. If you are a member of such a group, bring this book to the members' attention and suggest putting it on the schedule. Start out with a commitment to three or four meetings to discuss various chapters and practices. The book group can then assess the value of these discussions, and decide whether to extend the topic of appreciation.

- Form a family appreciation group. Use the chapters and practices in this book as the content. One important guideline: make membership voluntary. Those family members who opt in are the right people to begin with. If others eventually get the vibe, invite them in and welcome them.

3. For more intensive support, form an accountability partnership with a family member, friend, or work associate. Meet periodically to discuss chapters in the book, experiment with its practices, make commitments to incorporate certain practices (or variants that you create) in your respective lives, and report back about how you did. Reviewing your experience and receiving enthusiastic support for progress from your accountability partner are enjoyable aspects of such a partnership. More importantly, they will strengthen your appreciative habits and skills.

4. If you feel truly finished with the book, do whatever's next for you. The Buddha urged his followers to treat the dharma (the Buddha's teachings) as a raft. When it has taken you to the other shore, it's time to put down the raft and continue walking on the path you find yourself on. Ask yourself, "What am I now ready for? What will further my growth? What will keep

me alive, vital, and continuing to deepen as a person?" If you're not sure of the answers, discuss it with someone whose listening ear and wise counsel you have come to trust. If this person's reflections and suggestions resonate with you, adopt them. Do what feels right.

Whatever you do, continue on your path of appreciation. There's no going back. It's like those sharp iron spikes at the entrance to parking garages. Heed the sign that reads "Warning! Severe tire damage if you back up!" Also, even if you don't back up, don't stay in one place for too long. Like a whale, if you stop moving, you might find yourself dead in the water.

So, keep moving. Keep learning. Keep appreciating. And keep growing.

References

Armstrong, Jim (2006). *Beyond the Mission Statement: Why Cause-Based Communications Lead to True Success.* Paramount Market Publishing, Inc.

Bennett, Hal Zina (2001). *Write from the Heart: Unleashing the Power of Your Creativity.* New World Library.

Bryant, Fred B., and Joseph Veroff (2006). *Savoring: A New Model of Positive Experience.* Lawrence Erlbaum Associates.

Cannon, Jimmy (1978). *Nobody Asked Me but: The World of Jimmy Cannon.* Holt, Rinehart and Winston.

Deroo, Carlene, and Carolyn Deroo (2006). *What's Right with Me? Positive Ways to Celebrate Your Strengths, Build Self-Esteem & Reach Your Potential.* New Harbinger Publications, Inc.

Frankl, Victor E. (1959). *Man's Search for Meaning.* Washington Square Press.

Fredrickson, Barbara L., and Marcial F. Losada (2005). "Positive Affect and the Complex Dynamics of Human Flourishing." *American Psychologist,* Vol. 60, No. 7, 678–686.

Howell, John (1989). *Happiness is an Inside Job.* Resources for Christian Living.

180   *Appreciative Moments*

Kabat-Zinn, Jon (1994). *Wherever You Go, There You Are* Hyperion.

Kelm, Jacqueline B. (2005). *Appreciative Living: The Principles of Appreciative Inquiry in Personal Life.* Venet Publishing.

Kinder, George (1999). *The Seven Stages of Money Maturity: Understanding the Spirit and Value of Money in Your Life.* Delacorte Press.

Kinder, George, and Susan Galvan (2006). *Lighting the Torch: The Kinder Method™ of Life Planning.* FPA Press.

Klontz, Ted, Rick Kahler, and Brad Klontz (2005). *The Financial Wisdom of Ebenezer Scrooge: 5 Principles to Transform Your Relationship with Money.* Health Communications

Kundtz, David J. (1998). *Stopping: How to Be Still When You Have to Keep Going.* Conari Press.

Lamott, Anne (1995). *Bird by Bird: Some Instructions on Writing and Life.* Anchor Books.

Levoy, Gregg M. (1997). *Callings: Finding and Following an Authentic Life.* Three Rivers Press.

Muller, Wayne (1999). *Sabbath: Restoring the Sacred Rhythm of Rest.* Bantam Books.

Rath, Tom, and Donald O. Clifton (2004). *How Full Is Your Bucket: Positive Strategies for Work and Life.* Gallup Press.

Remen, Rachel Naomi (1997). *Kitchen Table Wisdom: Stories That Heal.* Riverhead Press.

Remen, Rachel Naomi (2000). *My Grandfathers Blessings: Stories of Strength, Refuge, and Belonging.* Riverhead Press.

Salmonsohn, Karen (2006). *Ballsy: 99 Ways to Grow a Bigger Pair and Score Extreme Business Success.* HOW Books.

Salmonsohn, Karen, and Don Zinzell (2001). *How to Be Happy, Dammit: A Cynic's Guide to Spiritual Happiness.* HOW Books.

Watkins, Jane Magruder, and Bernard J. Mohr (2001). *Appreciative Inquiry: Change at the Speed of Imagination.* Jossey-Bass/Pfeiffer.

Williamson, Marianne (1996). *Return to Love: Reflections on the Principles of a Course in Miracles.* HarperCollins.

About the Author

Writing *Appreciative Moments* has been a real adventure for me: full of joy, exhilaration, meaning, and the occasional frustrating obstacles that have led to creative growth. As I reflect on the process of birthing this book, I recall my elevator speech (discussed in chapter 22): "I bring all of myself to my work, so we may bring all of your *self* to life." This journey has called on me to summon everything I know, have experienced, and believe—all of myself—in the hopes of encouraging and guiding you to bring all of your *self* to life.

My work consists of the following services, to each of which I bring positive, strength-based, and practical approaches and methods, as well as all of myself.

- **Individual and Group Coaching:** business and personal coaching from an appreciative perspective

- **Organizational Consulting:** helping small businesses and mid-sized companies chart their mission and strategic courses, create life-affirming cultures, and work with greater effectiveness and meaning

- **Workshops and Keynotes:** bringing Appreciative Inquiry and positive psychology to life for attendees, to bring out their best, and to help them find their own ways to be their best, at work and in their personal lives

- **Staff Retreats and Client Events:** lively, informative events for connecting, celebrating, and appreciating the firm and its services

- **Client Tools and Newsletter Content:** AI-based questionnaires and interview guides for use with clients, and "Appreciatively Speaking©" columns for newsletters.

For further information, please contact me at Ed@EdwardJacobson.com, or go to www.EdwardJacobson.com.

I received my PhD in psychology from Indiana University and an MBA from the Wharton School. The numerous careers I draw on in my work include psychology professor, community mental health center executive, organizational consultant with a global consulting and accounting firm, and independent coach and consultant. These days, my greatest education comes from living with my wife, Jody, and stepson, Aman, in Madison, Wisconsin.

978-0-595-42911-0
0-595-42911-4

Made in the USA
San Bernardino, CA
11 March 2016